weddings with today's families in mind

D0907479

weddings with today's families in mind

a handbook for pastors

Doreen M. McFarlane

THE
PILGRIM
PRESS

Cleveland

To the memory of my beloved parents,
Eddie and Jean Borgfjord.
There was never a dull moment in their marriage
of almost fifty years,
but every moment was one of total commitment and love.

The Pilgrim Press, 700 Prospect Avenue,
Cleveland, OH 44115
thepilgrimpress.com
© 2007 by Doreen M. McFarlane

11 10 09 08 07 5 4 3 2 1

All rights reserved. Published 2007
♲ Printed in the United States of America
acid-free paper with 30% post-consumer fiber

Library of Congress Cataloging-in-Publication Data

McFarlane, Doreen M.
Weddings with today's families in mind : a handbook for pastors /
Doreen M. McFarlane.
p. cm.
ISBN 978-0-8298-1737-9 (alk. paper)
1. Marriage service. I. Title.
BV199.M3M34 2006
265'.5—dc22
2006100384

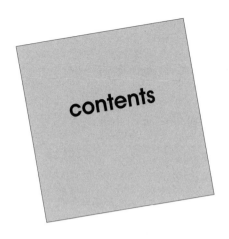

contents

preface

"How do I actually do a wedding?" has been the lament of almost every pastor I know. The wedding day is a profoundly important day for the couple and their families, yet most of us have never had any education at seminary—or anywhere else, for that matter—on how to perform this aspect of our work. Although bookstores have multiple wedding books for everyone from the bride and bridesmaids to the mother-in-law, there is little for clergy, especially when it comes to guiding us in handling the often difficult family situations that are part of today's weddings. And in this twenty-first century, there is no such thing as a typical wedding! Word and prayer resources are available, but there is little advice on how to deal with the delicate and highly important task of preparing, rehearsing, and officiating at today's unique weddings.

Most everything I share in this book has been gleaned from real life experiences; from mistakes, from successes, and from surprises—the kind of information and ideas that can come only from the doing! I've included some wedding scenarios that I think will touch your heart—or make you laugh! Throughout the book I've also interspersed theological reflections, not at the beginning of chapters as is the usual custom, but rather at the places they came to me in the process of writing. It is my hope that this more natural flow of ideas will bring us, writer and reader, closer to a real life conversation. I also think that this reflects the ways in which God often surprises us. Memories and reflections don't come "on schedule"; rather, they come to us in the midst of daily life.

Weddings with Today's Families in Mind goes a step beyond the typical wedding book, not only in its coverage of wedding preparation and procedures, but also because it was written with today's unique families in mind. I'll walk you through the couple's initial visit to your office, through the rehearsal and the wedding ceremony, all the way to the reception (should you choose to attend). I'll also address weddings with special circumstances and offer suggestions for wedding sermons.

I hope this book will help you become comfortable, proficient, and able to plan ahead to deal gracefully with whatever family issues may be facing you in the weddings at which you officiate. You may want to read the book straight through, or consult it about issues as they arise. Either way, I hope you will enjoy it. Let's be two neighboring pastors chatting over a cup of coffee in one of those rare afternoons that we get a moment from our busy schedules to stop, take a breath, and enjoy each other's company.

My deepest thanks go to The Pilgrim Press for its enthusiasm for my work. I especially thank my editorial director, Kim Martin Sadler, for her most gracious assistance, Pilgrim editor Timothy Staveteig for his early interest and continuing support of the project, and Marcia Broucek for her amazing editorial work.

I am most appreciative of friend and colleague Graydon Snyder for his encouragement and ideas on Free Church wedding possibilities as we wrote our previous book together. I thank the churches of Illinois, Florida, and Connecticut that I have served, and especially The Flagg Road United Church of Christ (Congregational) in West Hartford and its wonderful people whom I most recently served.

My deepest thanks go out as well to the many brides and grooms over the years in whose weddings I have participated as a vocal soloist and then, later, as a pastor. I am also grateful for the opportunity to meet and celebrate with their delightful families. They have touched my heart, my ministry, and my life. And, finally, my gratitude, respect, and love go to Michael McFarlane, my beloved husband, not only for his interest in this wedding project but, even more, for his continuing full support of my ministry, teaching, and love of writing.

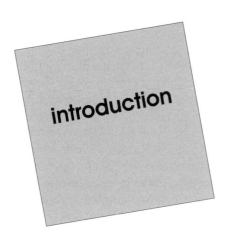
introduction

■ "the times they are a-changing"

The phone rings. On the other end of the line, an enthusiastic young adult, or maybe an older one, says something like this: "We're going to get married, and we would like you to perform the ceremony. I have to tell you, though, that my family situation is a bit complicated, but I'm sure you'll know what to do."

It is a well-kept secret that often we pastors, however experienced, respond with a deep-seated silent concern, thinking to ourselves, "Another wedding! How am I going to handle this one?" We want to be sure this couple's special day will become a beautiful memory, but little, if anything, we learned in seminary has prepared us for this aspect of our ministry. God help us!

Our concerns are not unfounded. The increasing variety of new family configurations and accompanying family dynamics in our modern times render our job more and more complex. Most of us have learned that, in this twenty-first century, there is no such thing as a typical wedding! Theologically educated, pastorally experienced, called and ordained though we pastors may be, it is clear that, when it comes to weddings in this era, our work is cut out for us.

Though weddings take place in settings anywhere from skydiving to scuba diving, couples still continue to come to the church, and to us as pastors, to be married, seeking to make their vows before Almighty God and gathered witnesses. And these couples often express the desire that their wedding be, at least in some ways, "traditional."

However, many (or maybe most!) of them have at least some family dynamics that do not fit into a category anything close to "traditional." In addition, there are bridal couples who are not church members and perhaps have not ever stepped inside a church. There are also an increasing number of intermarriages of all kinds: racial, religious, and cultural. And, of course, there is the relatively new matter of gay and lesbian weddings. (These are discussed in Part Three: Special Circumstances, but almost everything in the book can be adapted to gay and lesbian weddings.)

Every wedding is distinct, with its own special joys. And every wedding has some things that go wrong, things we can't predict until they happen. It is good for us as pastors to remind couples to celebrate every minute of their wedding day—*and* to expect glitches. We can reassure them that we will simply deal with these things and go on. Still, there are many difficulties that can be avoided when we pastors are well-prepared.

■ today's family dynamics

Certain events in life just naturally render hearts more tender and feelings more sensitive. Unfortunately, these same events also have the capacity to put everyone on edge. Rarely is there a day in life more potentially emotionally explosive than a wedding day. How often have you heard someone say, "I'll be fine if I can just get through the day of the wedding"?

And for good reason! People who might not otherwise choose each other's company are often thrown together at a wedding. Old memories and unforgiven mistakes might crop up. Or ex-spouses and estranged family members might show up. There are also the delicate issues of who will be asked—or not asked—to participate in various capacities.

As wonderful as they are for most who are involved, weddings are also a venue for the emergence of all manner of family issues. As a result of prior marriages—of the bride and groom, of their parents and relatives—many weddings (sometimes even wedding parties) include ex-spouses, as well as children or relatives from previous relationships. These people may get along well, but this is not always the case. Weddings present the potential for family members to be beleaguered by unpleasant emotions over old hurts, disappointments, and family controversies. By performing a well-organized wedding rehearsal and service, you can help make a wedding day the joyous day it was meant to be.

Weddings also present the potential for any number of family members to be overwhelmed—or at least not at their best. As the pastor, you can be a real help. By gleaning as much information as is appropriate in advance from the bridal couple, by leading a well-planned, family-friendly wedding rehearsal and ceremony and, most of all, by being sensitive to all persons involved, you can guide everyone with grace through the day. You can also help prevent misunderstandings that might otherwise cause family problems that could go on for generations.

In years past, we could simply consult a book on etiquette to learn the protocol for weddings. Everyone knew, for instance, that the father walked the bride down the aisle to meet her awaiting groom. Today, a bride might choose from several options. She and the groom may choose to enter together, or she may walk the aisle alone. When asked, "Who gives this woman to be married to this man?" the father used to answer, "I do." Now, if the question is even asked, there are many choices of response. In the past, everyone knew children arrived "after" the wedding. Today, children of the bride, the groom, or both are often participating in the ceremony.

Nearly all the *traditions* have become *options*, and the whole business of getting married has become more complex. This is the age of so-called blended families: with divorced and remarried family members at all levels, children with only one parent or many parents, and brides and grooms who may have two or even three people they call Mom or Dad.

It may not be possible to keep every person at the wedding happy, although we can certainly try. We as pastors can make a big contribution, facilitating a day of beautiful memories for couples and their families, by being aware of needs and sensitive to today's family dynamics.

remembering the priority

Although, ideally, every person should have a good experience at the wedding, the primary focus will always be on the bridal couple. The couple's covenant-making is the principal reason for the day. Still, their happiness on that day will be affected by the joy and good experiences of every person they love who is present at the wedding. Our caring presence with their loved ones and friends at this important time in their lives will mean a lot to them.

Couples do not always realize it, but they will likely end up being the host and hostess of the wedding event. In years past, it was most often the bride's parents who had that role, but today more and more the couple takes on the responsibility of making all the arrangements, and family and friends expect them to be sure everything goes well and everyone has a good time. This places a large burden of responsibility on the couple, and it is very easy for one or both of them to feel overwhelmed by the double responsibilities of the vows being made, along with the hosting of a party for everyone they love and care about. Although we pastors do not take on specific hosting responsibilities, there are ways we can help the couple get through the day with grace. For starters, we can help them concentrate on what is most important, to ensure that the focus of the day is to honor their relationship and celebrate their vows.

As pastors, we see the wedding as a step in the couple's faith journey and as their opportunity to make lifetime promises to each other. Some couples will understand more than others the significance of their decision to have a religious wedding. Either way, we can help them understand the importance of their choice.

If the couple are young people whom you and your church have nurtured since childhood, or if you know either the bride or the groom well, you probably will have some opinions as to the wisdom of that person's choice for a life partner. This, of course, is not your business. In my entire internship year in preparation for ordained ministry, probably the best advice I got from my senior pastor colleague was something that went like this: "Don't ever try to talk them out of getting married. There is nothing you can say that would make a bit of difference. Once they arrive at your door to talk about a wedding, there *will* be a wedding, whether it is at your church or somewhere else. Say yes and then give them a good experience of God. They will remember that."

On the other hand, the bride and groom may be total strangers to you and to the church. If you agree to perform their wedding, there is always a possibility that they might later choose to join your church, stay, and raise their family there. The wedding provides an excellent opportunity for the couple to get to know you as a pastor, to experience the church you serve, possibly to meet church members and learn more about the faith. It is often the case that couples who are married in a particular church, or even in a park or home by a Christian pastor, will return later when a child is to be baptized or brought to Sunday school. They may return and stay!

Still, more often than not, new couples coming to your church for the first time to be married will probably perceive you and your church as being "hired" to provide a service. Depending on how many meetings or marital counseling sessions you and/or your denomination require, they may decide to go elsewhere after their initial visit with you. Their decision will often depend on their initial motives for seeking out a church wedding and will likely *not* be a reflection on your words or behavior. For example, they may want a church wedding only to fulfill some dream about what the wedding is to look like. (Their disappointment if the church doesn't have a center aisle for the processional is often a strong clue!) Or it may be that, at some unspoken level, one or both members of the couple is truly seeking a closer relationship with God, or seeking a way to find faith. It is our responsibility as pastors to always keep this possibility in mind.

Either way, it is important that they have a good church experience. True, they may or may not have chosen you and your church for the right reasons. Perhaps they even found you in the yellow pages. Whatever their reasons, it is you they have chosen. You will now be sharing with them one of the most important days of their lives, and that is always a privilege.

■ you, the pastor, as facilitator

Once it is agreed that the wedding will take place, it becomes your responsibility as the pastor to act as religious leader, guide, and facilitator. Even if you were secretly reluctant to perform the wedding—for any number of reasons—once you have agreed to do it, then do it with all your heart. Decide in advance approximately how much time you will be spending on the preparation and on this wedding, and tell the couple what the requirements and costs will be, up front. Then follow through. Every wedding is another chance for you, the pastor, to grow in this particular skill. The more complex the family situation, the more experience you will get! And, in facilitating this very important event in each couple's life, you will have the opportunity to communicate to them the love of God, as well as the caring atmosphere of your particular church community. A wedding in which a Christian pastor is officiating, whether or not it takes place in the church, will always be a service of worship.

You, the pastor, are called to guide, move, prod, and help the bride, groom, participants, and the family to help make this the day everyone hopes it will be. Some wedding books, for example, suggest that a wedding coordinator will organize and conduct the wedding rehearsal. This is simply not the case. Under nearly all circumstances, you, the pastor, will be conducting the rehearsal, although a coordinator, a church wedding committee, or some family member may assist.

As you read this book, consider the particular gifts you as pastor bring to the wedding scene and to the families involved. These include your church's theology and ways of worship, as well as your own personality and ministerial style. Once you have learned to be comfortable with both the little details and the big picture, those gifts that are uniquely yours will be able to come to the fore and will bless everyone involved.

As you put the ideas in this book into practice, continue to think about your unique style, and how your gifts could be employed to help make weddings truly family-friendly. Here are some questions that might help you honor and utilize your style:

- Am I a warm and caring person, and does it show when I'm with people?
- Am I good at directing groups of people in a way that makes them comfortable?
- Do I remember names and faces?
- Am I good with children?
- Do I engender confidence in others?
- Do I prepare and deliver a sermon or meditation that is meaningful to everyone present?
- Am I a good counselor?
- Am I well-organized?

Each of us has different talents to offer, so do not be discouraged if you simply don't shine in some of these areas. Some can be learned. Others will just fall into place as you get more comfortable in what you are doing. Ultimately, your way of conducting wedding rehearsals and weddings will depend upon your personal style and temperament.

Still, it is good to remember that strong but sympathetic and caring direction is needed and much appreciated throughout the process. You are neither a buddy nor a dictator; people don't like to be pushed, but they do like to know someone is in the leadership position. They want to be reassured that you know what you are doing! If you handle things with confidence, the couple and everyone in the family and bridal party can relax more and enjoy the proceedings.

The pastor's role at the wedding rehearsal might be described as something like a compassionate stage director, someone with dignity and a sense of humor. The pastor is also a caring and qualified representative of the church. The couple will always remember how you treated them and how you related to those they love, especially the most vulnerable among their family and beloved friends. They will recall how you carefully guided them through the wedding preparations. They may not remember exactly what words you said at the wedding ceremony itself, but they will remember you as the facilitator of the setting in which they made their promises before their God and loving witnesses.

part one

preparation
for the
wedding

1 meeting with the couple

■ the two & their relationship

THEOLOGICAL REFLECTION
Marriage is a holy and honorable estate, ordained by God. It should not be entered into unadvisedly or lightly, but reverently, discreetly, advisedly, soberly, and in the fear of God.—The Book of Common Prayer

Although, we might assume that a couple knows all of the above before the wedding, these traditional words from the Episcopal *Book of Common Prayer* are still powerful and important. It might be good to read them—or something similar from your tradition—to the couple at their first premarital session, if not at the wedding itself. The words are valuable for many reasons. First, they remind the couple that society and God do view marriage not only as honorable but also as holy. What could be more holy than two people's loving commitment to each other for a lifetime? The words also remind couples of the absolute seriousness of the marriage vows. Each person is to enter into the marriage reverently, discreetly, advisedly, and soberly. And, finally, the phrase "in the fear of God" reminds the couple that they will not face life alone, that God will be with them in all that life brings.

As pastor, you will be deciding how many premarital sessions you will want to conduct with the couple, as well as how much of your time together will be spent on preparation for the couple's life ahead and how much will be devoted to practical plans related to the wedding ceremony itself. (Although I'll touch on premarital counseling, the book's primary focus is on how you can best meet the needs of the couple and their family members at the rehearsal and during the day of the wedding.)

Your premarital meetings will help you find out more about these people as a couple, and about their relationships with their respective family members. In hearing and observing how the bride and groom deal with their own families and with each other's family situations, you will learn some important information about the couple. This will help with any marriage-related counseling you might propose to them. The marriage counseling portion of your time with them might include such matters as the meaning of marriage as covenant, their compatibility, dealing with conflict and financial issues, and, if they are members or will be members of the church you serve, their role as a new family in the congregational life.[1]

Many pastors do not feel fully qualified or even comfortable in their role as marriage counselor. It is perfectly acceptable, and often better, to recommend other professional counselors who can do some high-quality counseling in advance of the wedding, especially in the area of advising—or even inquiring—about the couple's current or future sex life. Too many times young couples are embarrassed and not helped when local pastors take it upon themselves to ask a lot of personal questions and try to advise in this area of their expertise (or lack thereof).

You will also want to gather the practical information needed to prepare for the wedding itself, such as:

- number of guests
- approximate percentage of guests who will be the bride's family and friends, and who will be the groom's
- the family configurations (parents, siblings, relatives, any previous marriage partners and members of those families)
- musical preferences (so they can choose their wedding music from available options)

- favorite and appropriate scriptural choices
- who will participate in what capacity (including everyone's first and last names, and who is related to whom)
- who will "give away bride" (more about that later!)

This is also a good time to give the couple some information about fees and any special church regulations. (The fees and information will most likely have been agreed upon by your church's governing board. It is helpful if this information is printed on a card for easy reference. You can give the card to the couple when they first inquire.)

It is also important that you speak quite firmly with the couple about the importance of bringing the marriage license, preferably to the rehearsal. It is easy, with all the excitement of the wedding day, for them to forget this very important item! Make it clear: No license, no wedding—no exceptions.

■ families in the wedding party or attending the wedding

As pastors, every one of us has probably faced every combination imaginable. While I can't cover every situation, I hope this section will help you consider how best to relate to the bride's and the groom's relatives who will be at the wedding: fathers (birth, adoptive, and stepfathers); mothers (birth, adoptive, and stepmothers); siblings (birth, adoptive, and stepsisters and stepbrothers); grandparents, greatgrandparents, aunts, uncles, cousins; special friends who will be attending the wedding; and perhaps even the couple's own children or ex-spouses. Every family dynamic will be different.

PARENTS

Today we cannot assume bride and groom will each have one mother and one father. Any number or combination of birth, step-, and adoptive parents may be present at the wedding. It is good to be prepared so you can welcome them and make them feel comfortable. (See also "seating immediate family members" on page 49. This may be an area you want to address early on.)

BIRTH PARENTS

If the bridal couple has birth parents only, then there will likely be fewer issues to deal with. In today's world, however, it is more often the exception than the rule that both the bride and the groom have both birth parents alive, well, married to each other, and coming to the wedding!

For most parents, the wedding of a beloved child is deeply emotional. For so many years, they have loved and nurtured this person who is about to be a bride or groom. The couple is going to make promises for a lifetime, go out into the world, and become a new family.

While there is usually joy over this new beginning, there is bound to be—spoken or unspoken—a sense of wrenching away from the family of origin. Parents are likely to be quite emotional about this event, whether they show it overtly or not. They may manifest their feelings in any number of ways. They may be controlling without realizing it. They may be weepy or very sensitive. They may behave strangely. It's good if you and the bridal couple can try to give parents what they need in order to get through this emotional day, as long as it doesn't cause a problem for the couple. But don't lose sight of the priority: This day is for the couple.

There is another type of birth parent to consider if the bride or the groom has been adopted. The birth parent may have been a virtual stranger as the child was being raised but now is requesting to attend the wedding. If the couple is expecting such a parent at the wedding, it's good to decide in advance where this person will be seated. If this person has not been a part of the child's life up until now, there is no obligation to offer a role in the wedding. This estranged parent may also be hurting a lot and in need of some tender care. A few careful words from a kind pastor, namely you, will surely be in order. It can often take real courage for this person to come at all. On the other hand, if the bride or groom do not want this person at the wedding, that is their call and needs to be respected.

STEPPARENTS

Most of us have heard people jokingly (or not so jokingly) refer to their stepmother as "my stepmonster." Even at the best of times, and in the finest of circumstances, being a stepparent is not easy. In many cases the stepparent and child are strangers thrown together simply as a result of two people falling in love. It is exceedingly difficult in most cases for a stepparent to take the place of any birth parent or beloved adoptive parent. But when the time comes for their stepchildren to become brides or grooms, stepparents may be no less emotional than a birth parent. Yet the stepparent does not always have the same role to play at the wedding. The stepparent is in a sensitive situation—or at least may feel that way.

Needless to say, every family situation is different. The stepparent may have entered into the family to replace a beloved spouse who had died. Or the birth parents may have divorced, and the children have only reluctantly accepted this new person into their family. Sometimes a stepparent is footing the bill for the wedding. Other times, the wedding is being paid for by the bride and groom themselves, or by some other parent or relative. Sometimes a bride's or groom's birth parent is present at the wedding as well as the stepparent, and each will have to find his or her appropriate place in the proceedings. Given how common divorces and remarriages are in today's world, you will likely encounter any or all of the following family members:

STEPFATHER OF THE BRIDE: If the stepfather is the only father known to the bride and is loved by her, the bride will very likely ask him to walk her down the aisle (more about this in Part Two). If, on the other hand, she has a birth or adoptive father with whom she is close, then she may choose that father to do the honors. Where does this leave the stepfather? If he loves the bride as a father, he will certainly be present at the wedding. He will also be there as husband of her mother, and that, in most cases, will be enough. He may or may not be asked to do anything "official" and that is all right. Still, the couple may do well to give him some task to perform or ask him to say a few words at the reception.

STEPFATHER OF THE GROOM: The stepfather of the groom may, likewise, have no explicit role in the wedding ceremony or reception, but he is there to celebrate the marriage of his wife's son. He also is there to accompany the groom's mother, his partner. That is his primary role and an important one. Again, he may be asked to help out in some specific way.

STEPMOTHER OF THE BRIDE: The stepmother of the bride has a similar role. It is unlikely that she will have a particular part in the wedding if the bride's mother is alive, loved, and present. She will attend, rather, as the wife of the bride's father and should be seated shortly before the wedding ceremony begins. If she and the bride's father have children together, or if any of her relatives are present at the wedding, they might be encouraged to sit with her.

If the bride's father is taking the bride down the aisle, then he and his current wife (the bride's stepmother) will be separated for a short time. As soon as he has brought his daughter, the bride, down the aisle and responded to the pastor's question "Who gives this woman?..." then he will immediately come and sit beside his current wife where a place has been kept for him and where he will remain for the rest of the ceremony.

STEPMOTHER OF THE GROOM: Similarly, the stepmother of the groom will not likely have a specific role in the wedding if the groom's mother is alive and present. And if the stepmother married the groom's father in circumstances that were less than "acceptable" to the rest of the family at the time—and the family still feels this way—then she may be somewhat uncomfortable but still expected to attend the wedding. Under these circumstances, the best the stepmother can do is get through the day and evening with grace. Your kindness to those second (and sometimes third) wives and husbands who may look a bit uncomfortable will go a long way toward keeping everybody feeling more relaxed.

ADOPTIVE PARENTS

In most cases, adoptive parents' situations will be the same as that of birth parents except that they have *chosen* their children or, at the least, their children have been chosen for them. They have loved these kids from the beginning, whenever that beginning was. Sometimes, however, both adoptive parents and adopted children are more sensitive to or easily hurt by various family situations, secretly wondering if things are being done in certain ways *because* they are the adoptive or adopted ones. Such feelings are rarely expressed in words but can still be present.

The bride, for example, may have a mother who adopted her at age ten but also have a living birth mother who raised her until that time. The bride will, in this case, have to decide which of the two will stand as her official "mother of the bride" for the wedding. In most cases this choice will be an obvious one for the bride, and not an issue for you to have to consider as the pastor. Still, if more than one "mother" will be attending the wedding, it is good for you to know in advance to avoid any embarrassing gaffs.

SCENARIO

One bride invited the following to her wedding: the person everyone thought was her birth father, her actual birth father, an ex-stepfather who had raised her from the age of six, and her current stepfather. When she arrived at the pastor's office, she had not yet been able to decide which, if any, of the four men would walk her down the aisle. She also hadn't decided what role the other three men might take in the wedding or reception.

The pastor had a chat with her about her relationships with all four of the "fathers," inquiring about the roles each had played in her life and how she related to them at the time, and currently. The pastor also helped her consider what their feelings about her were, as well as the practical aspect of giving serious respect to the one who was paying for the wedding. In addition, the pastor asked her to bear in mind:

- how each of these men might react to whatever role she would assign to him in the wedding
- how the related mothers or spouses might feel about that role
- how the groom might feel about the bride's decision

- most importantly and ultimately, what the bride really wanted

The key for a pastor in this situation is not to decide for the bride, or even try to head her in any particular direction, but simply to be a good listener. This is her wedding and her life. Ultimately, it is her choice.

EX-SPOUSES

It is unlikely, but certainly possible, that the bride or groom will want to invite an ex-spouse—or even ex-spouses—to the wedding. It does happen! Although many couples who are no longer married to each other consider their "ex" as an enemy, or at best someone they would prefer not to see, there are also ex-spouses who remain friends. This is often the case because of children whom they share, so the adults have worked hard to get along with each other. Or they may value their shared history, even some good memories. If both bride and groom are comfortable with the presence of the ex-spouse, then why not?

It goes almost without saying, however, that if either the bride or groom is thinking of inviting an ex-spouse to the wedding, the new partner needs to be comfortable with this plan. The feelings of the new spouse in this regard are much more important than those of any "ex." The couple will also need to consider any discomforts the "ex" may experience, as well as any spouse, fiancé or fiancée, or special friend whom the "ex" might bring to the wedding. Whatever the arrangement, there is little doubt that an "ex" will experience considerable emotions, either positive or negative, at the wedding. As the pastor, you might want to have a few words with him or her to make them feel welcome, as well offer a listening ear.

GRANDPARENTS, GREATGRANDPARENTS & STEPGRANDPARENTS

To make a very broad generalization, it may be said that grandparents and greatgrandparents of all types are usually in good spirits at the wedding. When one's children's children are getting married, it is very likely a time to relax. Grandparents are usually at the point of life where they can feel proud without having to take on a lot of responsibility (emotionally or financially) or to worry too much about how the wedding will turn out. Hence, they will likely, if their health is decent, be able to have a good time. At weddings, grandparents will be remembering not only their own marriages but those of their children, so this is a time for memories and deep emotions—feelings that have mellowed through the years. As pastor, it is good to take a few minutes to ask these older people how they are enjoying the wedding. They will love telling you.

THOSE WHO HAVE TRAVELED TO THE WEDDING

Often these "elders" will have traveled some distance to the wedding, and possibly at considerable expense. If they have health issues, there will have been some cost of physical discomfort as well. There will be certain expectations, no doubt, on their part of the "paying of respects" by all concerned. At a minimum, grandparents and greatgrandparents need to be given special seating at both the church and the reception. As the pastor, you might also gently suggest to the bridal couple that they find a place during the wedding in which they can verbally acknowledge the efforts of these elders who have come, and celebrate their presence.

SOME AGE-RELATED MATTERS

While today's grandparents are often younger and healthier than in the past, this is not always the case. Sometimes grandparents and greatgrandparents will come to a wedding even though they're in very poor health. In fact, they may even have been working hard at staying alive just for this occasion! You might suggest to the bridal couple that someone in the family keep an eye on them in order to assist them through the wedding day. (The bride and groom will simply be too busy.) If any of these elders have trouble hearing, let the couple know if your church offers hearing devices. If they are in wheelchairs, you as the pastor will know the best spot for them to be seated for a good view of the ceremony, easy access to restrooms, and such. Tell the couple at the outset whether your church is handicapped accessible.

SCENARIO

A couple was deeply in love and became engaged. They wanted to commit for a lifetime. The next step? A wedding? Well, maybe . . . As they began to think about making plans, things got a bit complicated. As it happened, he had one ex-wife and a daughter who lived with him half the time. His ex-wife was happily married, had two other children, and would probably not be interested in attending the wedding. His beloved twelve-year-old daughter might want to be a junior bridesmaid. So far, so good. Now, for the bride's family. She had a birth mother and stepfather, a father and two stepmothers by her father's second and third marriages. She had an older sister (her mother's other child) and a stepsister (her father's second wife's daughter.) These two sisters were estranged (another wedding related issue). In addition, her future husband's background was Roman Catholic but her mother was a Protestant pastor.

On top of the usual difficult decisions that have to be made for a wedding (such as what to wear and whom to invite), this couple had much more on their plate! Who would they choose for the bridal party? Who would even be willing to sit with whom at the reception? Who would perform the wedding? Which church? In addition, no one in this situation was coming to the fore to offer to help the couple with what looked like mounting expenses. They loved and respected everyone in their families, but in the end, they made a good decision for their future—they eloped! Everyone in the family received an announcement and, later, a set of really great photos of a wedding on the beach in the Caribbean. The couple was smiling, no one had been hurt—and they had a great vacation to boot!

◼ relatives who are disenfranchised

Disenfranchised relatives will usually not be expected to attend the wedding, but the fact is, sometimes they do. I'm talking about the relatives who, for whatever reason, have kept themselves removed by choice or by request of the family, but who occasionally show up at weddings and funerals. It is good if you, as pastor, know a bit about these people in advance of the wedding. That way, should they choose to turn up at the wedding, you may be able to diffuse any difficult or embarrassing situations.

The best way to find out about them in advance is to simply ask. When the couple is telling you about their families and giving the names of those who are to be in the wedding party, simply ask, "Are there any other relatives I should know about?" They might say something like this: "We do have an Uncle Fred, but be sure not to mention him at the wedding." Then you know: He'll be the one to watch for! And if good old Uncle Fred does decide to show up, there is no reason for you not to be decent to him. The problem is, after all, the family's problem, not yours. The family has probably been dealing with this recalcitrant relative for years, and they'll likely know how to handle any matters that may come up at the wedding.

◼ the business of the previous pastor, your predecessor

Ideally, church people would like it if their "new" pastor is a good friend to their retired pastor or earlier pastors who have moved on to other churches. Certainly this can happen but, when it comes to weddings, there is often a discomfort zone that has to be dealt with by all concerned. When people have been served by a beloved pastor for many years, they will very often ask for that person to officiate at their wedding service. Sometimes they will even come to you, the current pastor, and ask or even tell you that they want good old reverend "fill-in-the-blank" to perform the ceremony.

Your response will vary depending on the traditions and regulations of your own denomination and local church. There are a number of reasons for urging the couple not to have this pastor lead or even participate in the leadership. To begin with, this pastor has chosen to retire or has moved on, or for any number of reasons, might want to be remembered as before. Also, if the two who are to be married are members of your church, this is one of the family moments that afford you, as their pastor, the greatest opportunities to bond with them. Once this opportunity is lost, it can be more difficult for them to identify with you as their pastor. It is very likely that your predecessor will be happy to follow your lead and, if asked to officiate, will just say no.

After you have carefully and calmly explained all this to the couple, you might suggest that, if they feel especially close to the other pastor, they might simply invite the pastor to attend the wedding.

2. music matters

■ practical issues

Often a bride, groom, or both, will want a family member or close friend to perform some music at the wedding. It is best to get the approval of your church organist or music director and have arrangements made through that person, even if he or she is not actually going to be accompanying the performer. There are many practical reasons for this. Singers and instrumentalists come at all levels of professionalism, and no one wants to be embarrassed, least of all the bridal couple.

Another reason for this precaution is that people perform best when in their own "element." If they are professionals, there should be no problems. If they are amateurs, they may also be wonderful. Still, any number of things can go awry if not dealt with in advance of the wedding.

One contemporary problem has to do with the issue of recorded musical accompaniment on tapes or CDs for soloists. If this comes up, you will need to know:

- Do your church regulations allow for recorded music by people who are not actually present in the worship event?
- Does your church have the technical equipment and speakers to play this music?
- Does the live performer, for example a singer, require a microphone in order to be heard over this recorded music?

- Is the performer in possession of the required tape or CD accompaniment?
- Will the CD be programmed carefully in advance so it begins at the right song?
- Has the bridal couple chosen someone to run the CD player?

In most cases, depending on the traditions and practice of your church, it is best to keep all the music live. If accompaniment is required, it can be performed by the church organist, a pianist, or other instrumentalist or group. In many cases accompanists will rehearse with the soloist in advance of the wedding—but not necessarily during the wedding rehearsal. This can hold up the rehearsal. You might suggest that they practice immediately before the wedding rehearsal and then have only a short "run through" during the actual rehearsal. Regardless of when it happens, it is *always* good for them to go through the music together before the wedding service so that any problems can be resolved up front.

■ choices

There are two primary criteria for the choice of music for a wedding:

- Is the music appropriate?
- Does the couple like this music?

It is usually good to remind the couple that a wedding is a service of worship, not just a celebration of their love relationship. Some will ask for their favorite song, but if that song does not enhance worship, you might suggest that it could be performed to much greater appreciation at the reception.

Then there is the question of how much music is appropriate. Couples who are engaged in musical lives may want more than a couple who simply enjoy music as a background to their lives. The "usual" amount of music might be an organ prelude and postlude, a solo during the lighting of a unity candle, and possibly even one or two hymns if the couple thinks the gathered group is willing to sing. Some couples will want to include vocal or instrumental soloists, or groups such as a trio, quartet, sometimes even a choir.

3 potentially sensitive issues at the rehearsal

▪ getting off to a good start: knowing names, roles, relationships

THEOLOGICAL REFLECTION
But now thus says the Lord, he who created you, O Jacob, he who formed you, O Israel: Do not fear for I have redeemed you; I have called you by name, you are mine.—Isaiah 43:1

Names are very important. Since biblical times, names have represented power. For this reason, we are never really told the name of God; only that God's name in Hebrew means something like "I am who I am." When we know and speak people's names, we honor them and show that we see them as valuable children of God. All people like to hear their names spoken—and pronounced correctly (or if in print, spelled correctly). If you can call people in the wedding party by their names, even just their first names, they are sure to feel valued. Nobody expects you to remember a long list of names, but if you do the best you can with regard to names, people will appreciate your efforts.

The wedding rehearsal and the rehearsal dinner that follows can become wonderful memories for the bridal couple, attendants, and family if the rehearsal is handled professionally and sensitively by the pastor.

If the family members get along well with the pastor and respect the pastor's direction, the rehearsal is likely to go more smoothly. It is of primary importance that you as pastor are in reasonable rapport with every person in the bridal party. For starters, it is good to know who's who: what each person's role is in the wedding, and preferably what that person's relationship is with the bride, groom, or both. If you observe how each of these people relates to the bridal couple, you will find it easier to help these people with the job they have at the wedding.

As the pastor, you will be the one who sets the tone for the rehearsal. The bridal party will sense whether you have everything under control. It is your warmth, welcoming, and professionalism that will make a calm, smooth, and successful rehearsal possible, no matter how nervous or distracted people are when they arrive.

However, no matter how well prepared you are, or how much you have things under control, there are bound to be a few glitches.

IF SOMEONE IS LATE

Inevitably, one or more members of the bridal party are late for the rehearsal. It may be acceptable to wait up to ten minutes or so, but not longer. This is a good opportunity for you, the pastor, to graciously but strongly remind everyone in the wedding party about the importance of arriving at the church on time for the wedding. Then simply announce that you will be going ahead with the rehearsal.

Ask the couple to temporarily assign the late person's role to someone else as a stand-in for the rehearsal. (There is usually a family member or friend at the rehearsal just to "observe.") Ask that person, then, to bring the missing bridal party member up to speed once he or she arrives. Most often, the missing person can step into the line-up and be positioned easily with a few minor instructions.

IF THE BRIDE OR GROOM DOES NOT SHOW UP

If either the bride or the groom does not show up, after a reasonable amount of waiting, you might want to cancel the rehearsal and ask that everyone come a half hour before the wedding ceremony for a short run through. (It would also be a good idea to find out what problem caused them to miss such an important event!)

It is even possible for a wedding to take place with no rehearsal at all, but that tends to make everyone involved nervous. The best way to avoid tardiness for rehearsals and weddings is for you, as pastor, to make the importance of being on time a priority at your premarital counseling sessions. Also, even if everyone is on time for the rehearsal, mention again the importance of being on time for the wedding. That day, especially, any number of things can make people late.

SCENARIO

The pastor agreed to perform a wedding for a beautiful young couple who had recently arrived from South America. On the day of the wedding, everyone arrived pretty much on time; everyone, that is, except the bride. The people were seated and anxiously waiting. The soloist, who had prepared no less than three different Ave Marias (Gounod, Schubert, and Mascagni), was in his place in the choir loft. The groom was out in back with his mother, as this was the custom from his particular country. The groomsmen nervously paced. Yet the bride did not come and did not come. It was decided that the soloist should sing an Ave Maria or two to keep everyone settled. An hour-and-a-half and six Ave Maria's later (two of each!), the bride finally arrived, all beaming and full of excuses. The groom felt she was worth the wait, and the wedding took place as planned—almost two hours late. It is presumed that they lived happily ever after!

■ the rehearsal:
helping everyone prepare for the great day

Once everyone who is participating in the wedding has gathered for the rehearsal, seat them for a few opening words from you, the pastor. I highly recommend that you use your microphone. Everyone will hear the directions more clearly, and it also will give you a sense of some authority in what can often become a situation of too many "experts." (Practically all the people in the place will have some idea of how this wedding is supposed to go, based on their own wedding experiences.) Assuming that you and the couple have already decided what will take place at the wedding, it is best at this point that you be the primary speaker, guiding the bridal party through the rehearsal with a tone of kindly and experienced authority.

The first thing you need to do is get everyone's attention and ask politely for silence. Then begin:

- Greet all who are present, telling the group your name, introducing yourself as the pastor, and telling them that you will be performing the ceremony.

- Welcome them to the church and, if you can do it with a few words, tell them just a bit about this particular church and your denomination.

- Be sure you have each person connected with the correct name and role in the wedding, so you can say something like, "Which one is Mary? Oh yes, you are the maid of honor. Right?" It's okay to have this written on a paper or notepad; they'll be impressed that you care enough about them to know their names.

- Take a few minutes to acknowledge that you understand everyone is excited and will be wanting to talk during the rehearsal, but that there are two reasons why it is practical for them to listen carefully and not chat too much: One, they will get out of the church and off to the rehearsal dinner sooner; and, two, on the wedding day, they will be very clear about what they need to do.

- Assure them that they are free to ask any questions as the rehearsal proceeds.

- Remind them that, if everyone concentrates for these next thirty to forty-five minutes or so, there will be absolutely no reason to lose sleep tonight! This opportunity to walk through the service will clarify what everyone is doing and what is expected of them. This will help reduce their nervousness and go a long way toward helping them enjoy their role at the wedding.

- Then, simply go through the wedding service step-by-step. Take a look at Part Two "the wedding day" (page 45) for particulars you might want to highlight at the rehearsal.

- Use your sense of humor. (If you don't have one, get one. It's useful in the ordained ministry!) If you are enjoying the rehearsal, chances are the participants will enjoy it as well, and all concerned will leave the rehearsal with a sense of confidence about their role in the upcoming ceremony.

There are two additional issues that it are helpful to address at the rehearsal. One concerns the bride. Check to see what kind of gown she will be wearing and if she will be wearing a veil. Talk over how both will be handled so that there will be no unwelcome surprises. (See the "the bride's gown" in the unity candle section on page 63, and the discussion of the bride's veil in "you may kiss the bride" on page 73.)

The other concerns the groomsmen. Since groomsmen are often also the ushers at the wedding, it is a good idea to chat with them (and the groom and father of the bride) at the rehearsal, going over a few details on "walking down the aisle" etiquette, such as how to offer a woman your arm to guide her in and out of the sanctuary. If someone has not had much experience with this, he might hold his arm in such a way that the woman cannot put her arm through his. Suggest that each usher simply crook his arm and hold it open and downward in some tension. This not only produces a space for the woman to put her arm through, but it also makes everything look very attractive during the comings and goings of the event.

Not every groomsman will know what to do when he leads a single woman or a couple to their seats. A little practice session of this at the rehearsal will make a world of difference. Traditionally, the usher offers his arm to the woman and, if she is accompanied by a man, he simply follows behind. When the usher arrives at the pew row where she is to be seated, the usher allows her to slip her arm out and he stands, facing the pew that she is to enter, leaving enough space for her to go into the pew and sit down. Only when she has been seated (along with her partner if there is one) does the usher return to the narthex doorway to lead the next person or couple to a seat.

As pastor, with a bit of humor, you can make this little lesson into a bit of fun to lighten up from the seriousness of the rehearsal. Even the most experienced usher appreciates a bit of guidance.

◼ the rehearsal dinner (should you decide to go): some dangers & some solutions

You, as the pastor, are by no means required to attend the rehearsal dinner. Your choice to go is entirely up to you. Some people will invite you because they have read in some wedding book that it is the right thing to do, or they may invite you because you are pastor of their church. Or the couple may invite you because they really like you.

Unless you are the pastor of one or both of the bridal couple, there is no pressure to attend. In fact, at some rehearsal dinners the bridal party members like to let down their hair and kick up their heels a bit, and the pastor's presence may not add to the fun. Some rehearsal dinners are intended to be intimate meals for the close family members, so they may want to be "alone" together.

Also, most bridal couples generally want to think of you in the capacity of the pastoral office you hold, and it will be easier for them the next day at the wedding if you have not been out partying with them the night before. It is rarely a problem to simply and graciously decline an invitation to the rehearsal dinner. Listen to your instincts in deciding what is appropriate for each situation.

4. involving family in the wedding

■ joys & challenges of family in the wedding party

The bridal couple will likely have already made up their minds before they meet with you about who exactly is to be in the bridal party. Many couples choose to invite family members to be maids or matrons of honor, bridesmaids, best man, grooms-men, or ushers. Often they include the children of the family as junior bridesmaids, junior ushers, flower girls, or ring bearers.

Some will want only close friends or only family for emotional reasons. Others are thinking of practical aspects, such as how these people will be able to help them with the wedding plans and prewedding events. Sometimes (alas) the couple will choose people for their good looks or matching heights; in other words, how they will look in the bridal party "line-up" or for the photographs! There are as many reasons as there are couples for choosing the bridal party participants.

There are, of course, both joys and challenges involved when a couple chooses family members to be part of the wedding party. Encourage the couple to think not only of what is best for themselves but also for the others who will—or will not—be involved. For example, it might be difficult to have a sister as a bridesmaid if she lives some distance, or has a demanding job and can't take many days off. Or she might simply prefer to attend and enjoy the wedding of her beloved sister. There is no protocol or hard-and-fast rule that siblings must be in the bridal party, although it can be a good thing when circumstances are right.

■ more opportunities for family to participate

A busy and involved family member is generally a happy family member. Everyone wants to feel needed. And as each does his or her job, large or small, some responsibility is taken off the couple (and you), and the wedding is likely to go more smoothly.

For those family members who are not part of the actual wedding party, there are a number of ways to be useful and included in special and helpful activities. You might make some suggestions in this regard. Are there family members gifted in any way? Why not employ those gifts? There are any number of possibilities. You might want to offer a prepared list of these ideas to share with the couple when you first meet with them for the wedding preparation.

OFFER MUSIC

A family member might have the talent to sing or play an instrument at the ceremony. Be sure to check with your organist/choir director before arranging for a friend or family member to play any church instrument, to keep everyone in the loop. Organists nearly all prefer that others do not play the church's pipe organ, as the stops have been set a certain way. Also, it is a very expensive instrument and should not be handled by too many people. If an outsider is permitted to play, arrangements should be made to meet with the church organist in advance of the wedding.

Sometimes the family member's music might be more appropriate for the reception. If the reception is a tea in the church basement, for example, or a quiet refined event, then a harpist, or a violinist and pianist, or a string trio might be beautiful. (One caution about this, however, is that even the most refined reception can get pretty loud, and a harpist might not be heard.) If the family member is a member of a band, the band might be asked to play for dancing at a more lively reception. Do remind the couple that if singers or instrumentalists in the family are professionals, *even if they are family members*, remuneration should at least be offered. The performer(s) may choose to offer their music in lieu of a wedding gift, but payment should always be offered and, if accepted, paid in advance of their performance.

TAKE PHOTOS OR RUN THE VIDEO CAMERA

If the family member has particular technical skills, he or she might be asked to run the video camera or take formal or candid photographs. However, the bride and groom should be sure, in advance, about the quality of work that person can provide. It is very upsetting to realize, after the wedding, that Aunt Gertie or Uncle George forgot to take off the pause button on the video camera!

SCENARIO

Larry was a collector, and he had many collector friends. In most respects they were fine friends but, when it came. to their collections, some tended to be secretive, and they held very tightly onto their possessions. When Larry became engaged to Marsha and they decided to have a small wedding, they did not want to spend a lot of money for wedding photos. One of Larry's collector friends was known to do some photography, so they thought it would be nice to ask him to serve as their wedding photographer.

The friend took hundreds of photos on the wedding day. However, a couple of weeks later, he and Larry had a falling out over some small collector issue. The friend, now no longer a friend, chose to express his negative feelings toward Larry by withholding the precious photos.

For months Larry and Marsha pleaded and negotiated and waited and hoped things would be resolved, but they never saw their wedding photos. The couple was deeply hurt and disappointed that they ended up with no photographic record (except for a few candid snapshots

from family) of their happiest day. The so-called "friend"
felt that he had won, but when it came to the friendship,
everybody lost.

OFFER VISUAL ARTS

Is there a family member gifted in the visual arts? If the couple is
looking for a creative touch for their wedding, they might ask this
person to paint a mural to be placed in the sanctuary or behind a
head table at the reception. Or they might ask someone to do
drawings of the ceremony that can be sent to family or friends who
were unable to attend. Or perhaps someone could draw sketches or
cartoons of people during the reception and share the drawings
with the guests. Another possibility would be to make arrangements for a family member's paintings to be hung in some appropriate place in the church or reception hall as part of the décor for
the special day. (Obviously, this would have to be done in a way
that did not damage the walls.)

PRESENT A LITURGICAL DANCE

Liturgical dance by an individual or group is becoming increas-
ingly popular in churches (especially in African American
churches.) Dance affords the opportunity for all who are present
to experience this beautiful and freeing visual form of worship. It
might be possible to include a liturgical dancer or group as part of
the wedding ceremony. If the couple is interested, a dancer in the
family could coordinate with the person or persons providing the
music.

LIGHT OR EXTINGUISH CANDLES

A specially chosen family member might open the wedding by
lighting candles on the altar or communion table, and then extin-
guish them as the ceremony ends. This person should probably
practice at the rehearsal. Candles are more likely to light quickly
if they have been prelit and extinguished in advance of the service.
Be sure the person extinguishing the candles uses a snuffer. This
will prevent wax from dripping on altar cloths, furniture, or clothing.

SCENARIO

Marla was in her ministerial internship year when she almost burned down a church. It was an honest mistake. The senior pastor had given her the responsibility (and/or privilege) of waiting around after a rather large wedding that he had performed, so he could go home to enjoy his dinner. It had been a magnificent wedding. The special decorations had included twelve lit candles, enclosed in twelve glass globes, tied with bright red ribbons to poles on each side of the first six pews. It had looked lovely.

Now Marla's job, in principle at least, was to wait around until the bridal party and friends had exited the building, turn out the lights, and lock up. She went about her business, spent some time in her office, and puttered around in the church hall with some work for Sunday. After an hour or so, she wandered up to the sanctuary to turn out the lights. To her surprise, she realized that no one had blown out the candles.

It was an incredible mess. Some of the candles were still burning in pools of their own liquid wax. Others had extinguished themselves. All were hot and dripping down the poles onto the pews and the carpet. Marla tried to remain calm. She managed to clean things up in an hour or two, but she learned a valuable lesson that day: Unless there is a trustworthy and routined custodian on duty, the pastor needs to be sure the candles are put out immediately following the service.

A real disaster was avoided that day, and the lesson is this: Never allow the emotions of the day to distract you from the practical realities of the situation. We as pastors are always required to focus on the task at hand.

READ SCRIPTURE OR SOME OTHER CHOSEN TEXT

If a family member has clear diction and is not afraid to stand up in front of people to speak, the couple could invite this person to read scripture or a poem or any short prose that is appropriate and significant. It is usually a good idea for this person to read through the passage at the rehearsal, to become familiar with walking up to the podium or pulpit and using the microphone. Be sure, unless the sanctuary or other wedding venue is very intimate, to encourage the reader to use the microphone. Many people think they would be uncomfortable using a microphone and believe their voices are particularly resonant, so they don't need one. In almost all cases, this is not a good idea. Acoustics are seldom what the speaker thinks they are. Also, older people are likely to have trouble hearing a voice that is not amplified, especially when other voices are. The general rule is that if *anyone* is using a microphone, *everyone* who is speaking should use one. People tune in to a particular audio level.

At the rehearsal, the reader will also have a chance to check out the pulpit or podium. Shorter people tend to disappear behind large pulpits and podiums. If your church has a small box or platform on which the shorter reader can stand, you will want to offer it.

MONITOR THE GUEST BOOK OR A SIGNED PHOTO-POSTER

A family member, preferably one with an outgoing personality, can be given the honor of taking responsibility for the guest book, bringing it to each table at the reception to be sure everyone signs it and inviting each person to add a few words of congratulations.

Sometimes, instead of a guest book or in addition to one, the couple will have an enlarged engagement photo mounted on a wide white matting, with space for comments and signatures by all who attend the wedding.

Most couples will simply be too busy on the wedding day to take care of getting the signatures themselves, and they will greatly appreciate a family member who helps in this way.

BRING FOOD TO THE RECEPTION OR BAKE THE WEDDING CAKE

In general, catering a dinner or a buffet at the wedding reception, even for a very small wedding, is probably too much work for a family member or group of family members—if they want to also enjoy the wedding. Still, depending on who is catering the meal or buffet, it may be possible for a family member who is a good cook to participate in some way. This, of course, would have to be arranged in advance with those who are providing the food. For example, the family member may be able to bring appetizers or some special punch, a chocolate fountain, or trays of fruit. They may want to provide some special kind of food that is representative of the culture of the bride or groom. This would be especially appreciated by family.

Sometimes there will be a family member whose great pride is baking. If that person has made wedding cakes before, the couple might ask him or her to bake the cake. The person should be appropriately paid for this, as wedding cakes can be very costly to bake and involve a great deal of time. If a friend or relative is baking the cake, you might want to remind the bride and groom that the type of cake is *their* choice, and they will need to be very clear about what they want.

If providing food for the wedding is too big an effort, there is always the rehearsal dinner/party. This is where the family can shine in the food department. Instead of going to a restaurant, family will often gather in the home of parents or relatives for a buffet or even a sit-down dinner prepared by the family.

PROVIDE FLOWERS

An artistic family member or group might be asked to work with flowers for the sanctuary or the reception, or the bouquets for the bride and her attendants. Some may be in a position to provide flowers or plants from their own gardens, while others are especially good at choosing them from a florist or even local grocery store and arranging them in the sanctuary or reception hall. The couple will know who might enjoy such tasks. One caution for you as pastor to mention is that they need to keep water from dripping on the wood and on the carpets of the church—and on their wedding attire!

■ wedding programs or bulletins that include family names

There is rarely a set format for a printed wedding program. These programs, whether simple or complex, can be very creative and beautiful. Although most times the programs are produced at the church by the church secretary, it is possible to farm out that responsibility to family members who are capable and interested. An artistic family member might want to design a special and personal cover for the program, choose the paper color and texture, as well as special fonts and formats. Another family member may want to write a poem or choose a biblical passage for the program. (These may also be read at the service by a reader or by the entire congregation.)

On the left inside page of the program, on the back cover, or in an insert, the couple has the opportunity to list not only the members of the bridal party but every family member and friend who was part of making the wedding such a wonderful day. Those whose names appear are sure to feel honored to see their names "in print." It's a great way for the couple to let family members and friends know how much they are appreciated, and the wedding programs will become treasured souvenirs of the wedding for everyone.

One caution must be mentioned. If there is going to be a list of people in the wedding program, it needs to be complete and accurate. If any name is left out—or even if a name is misspelled—the affected family member may be offended. Remind the couple either to include *all* names or *no* names, and to check all spellings carefully.

One other thought about programs: A younger or physically challenged family member might enjoy handing out the programs as people enter.

■ remembering loved ones who have died, or who cannot attend

THEOLOGICAL REFLECTION

Therefore, since we are surrounded by so great a cloud of witnesses, let us . . . run with perseverance the race that is set before us . . . looking to Jesus . . . who, for the sake of the joy . . . endured the cross.
—Hebrews 12:1–2a

In some very powerful way, we are not alone with God when we worship: We are together with those who are in the sanctuary with us. The experience of worship also brings us into some holy connection with those we love who have gone before and, indeed, with all Christians who have passed on and are now with God. This is spoken of poetically in the Book of Hebrews as being present with "a cloud of witnesses." The Apostles' Creed refers to this experience as "the communion of saints." When worship happens (and a wedding ceremony is indeed a worship service), all of God's people, those alive now and those who have died, are gathered and truly present in a mysterious and beautiful way.

On almost every wedding day, along with the joy, there is usually some hint of underlying sadness—sadness for beloved family members or dear friends who have died. The couple and the gathered guests may be acutely aware of those not present to witness this sacred family event. This sadness can truly be turned to joy if a place can be found in the wedding service simply for their names to be spoken.

If those now passed away were parents or grandparents of the bride, they can be mentioned when the bride is being "given in marriage," something like this:

Pastor: "Who gives this woman to be married to this man?

Father: "Her mother and I, along with our dear parents and grandparents who have gone before us."

This kind of response communicates the profound idea that the bride's entire family of origin is, in some mysterious way, present in worship, celebrating with her as she journeys into her new life, and that the entire family gives its blessing, even if some are in absentia.

A second option would be for the family to share a treasured story about the person who has passed away. If the story is appropriate, it might be included in the sermon or meditation or given as a reading by a family member.

A third possibility is for you as pastor (or another chosen person) to announce that the upcoming scripture reading, poem, solo, or hymn was a favorite of the bride or groom's deceased grandparent (or whatever family member).

Any of these acts of memory will bring about a sense of "the communion of the saints."

There are also times when someone who is dearly loved and still alive is simply unable, for reasons of health or other causes, to attend the wedding, Any of the above options could be employed, so that this person will be remembered and included. The mentioning of the person's name at the ceremony, with the person's knowledge (and their permission of course), will have an impact.

When bridal couples tell you how much they wish this person or that relative could come to the wedding, encourage them to explore these possibilities to include that person in the ceremony.

* * *

Congratulations! You've made it through another wedding rehearsal. No noses out of joint! No family arguments! Nobody upset with the pastor! And all of the bridal party will sleep well tonight knowing their roles are clear and they have been rehearsed. If your sermon is prepared, you, too, will rest easy. You are ready now for Part Two—the day of the (perfect?) wedding.

part two

the
wedding day

5 before the ceremony: setting the scene

◼ helping the bridal party & family stay on track

The day has arrived, you have arrived at the church (or whatever venue has been chosen for the ceremony), and the bridal party begins to arrive—in good time, if all is going well. If the service is at your church and your custodian does not work that day, you may need to come early enough to unlock the doors, turn on the lights, and be sure the heat or air conditioning is on.

In the half hour or so before the service, it is a good idea to simply walk around, checking to make sure everything is falling into place and that people are approximately where they need to be. Here is a short checklist:

- Are the flowers set in the right places and not in the way of the procession or ceremony?
- Are candles prepared and any altar cloths and such set in place correctly?
- Are matches or the candle lighter in place or in the hands of the people who will need them?
- Is the organist and any other instrumentalists or singers present and ready to go? Do they have a copy of the program?

- Are the bulletins being handed out and people being directed to their seats?
- Are the microphones turned on? Have any required batteries been checked?
- Have the immediate family members arrived, as far as you know?
- Are all the members of the bridal party present and accounted for?

If the bride is tradition-oriented, she may not want the groom to see her until she comes down the aisle. Some larger churches offer a bridal room, but most do not. You will have arranged in advance whether or not the women will dress at the church. Depending on the weather, it may be a practical idea for them to do so. If your worship place does not offer a bride's room, it may be practical for the bride and her attendants to gather in your study/office. If you have offered your space, you might as well be gracious, make them welcome, and get out of the way. Be sure that any purses, bags, or other valuables belonging to the wedding party are either locked up in your office or elsewhere before the service begins. Better yet, ask the couple to choose someone not in the wedding party to be assigned the job of keeping guard over purses, bags, and valuables in the sanctuary. That way you won't have to go looking for the people to return their belongings when you want to close up your office and leave. Even if your church has never experienced a robbery, there is always a first time. Because events such as weddings are often posted in local newspapers, churches can become targets of thieves during weddings.

Once you have determined that everything is in its place and all the main people expected by the family have arrived, you are almost ready to enter the sanctuary with the groomsmen and groom (if this is the type of processional they have chosen—more on that point below). Be sure that, in the excitement of the moment, you have not forgotten to bring your own Bible and any notes for the service, as well as your copy of the program. Before you proceed into the sanctuary, it is important to give some individual attention to both the bride and the groom.

some private words of wisdom to the bride

What you say to each bride will depend a lot on the individual, on what you've learned about her through the counseling period, and also on the mood she seems to be in immediately before the wedding. It will also depend to some degree on how many people are gathered around her, and who these people are. You might take the bride aside and tell her warmly that you'd like to have just a few minutes with her alone.

Remind her, as you will also remind the groom, that the moments ahead may well be some of the happiest memories of her life, so she should treasure them. She may be very nervous. If so, it is good to diplomatically suggest that she try not to be concerned from this point on with matters over which she has no control, such as her gown or how she or anyone else looks. Remind her that these moments ahead are between herself and her beloved and God, not about how others are responding to the wedding. Tell her, too, that you, as the pastor, are really only the facilitator of those special moments, and that the guests who are assembled are present as loving, caring witnesses who have come to offer their blessings.

These are only suggestions of what you might want to say to each bride because, of course, every couple and every wedding is different. Ultimately, it is the fact that you take these few minutes with the bride that counts.

and words for the groom

Take the opportunity as well to go to the groom and offer a few similar words. It is often appropriate to begin light-heartedly because the groom is nearly always surrounded, at this time right before the wedding, by his buddies in the bridal party. Depending on the state of mind of the groom, you may or may not want to joke with him by asking—with a smile—if he still wants to go through with it! All bets are that he will always say yes. (I have not included advice as to what to do if a groom says no, but it's not likely to happen.)

Try to get the groom alone, even if it's just for a minute or two. Your few words can help him focus on the profound wonder of what is about to take place. Remind him, as you did the bride, that this will be his time with his beloved and with God. Suggest that he relax, enjoy, and really take in the moments ahead. They are memorable moments that will affect the rest of his life.

SCENARIO

Eddie had avoided getting married all these years. He was thirty six when he met Jean, and he knew right away that she was the one. Still, he was well aware of the dangers. Would she always love him? Would he really be able to provide for a wife and the children they would share? Was he making a mistake?

The wedding was at his sister's home. He and his best man were sent to the basement until time for the ceremony, as it was considered bad luck to see the bride before the wedding.

The best man asked him, "So, are you ready to get married?"

Eddie looked up at the one very small basement window and answered, "Do you think I could crawl out that window?"

A few minutes later the pastor arrived and decided to go down to the basement and see how the "boys" were doing. He, too, asked Eddie, "So, are you ready to get married?"

This time the answer changed. Eddie's words were these: "Well, Pastor, I believe I am."

This particular marriage lasted forty-nine love-filled years.

---

6 family-focused seating plans

Traditionally, the groomsmen serve as ushers before they take their place in the ceremony, but there may be additional or separate ushers. The ushers' job is to stand in the narthex of the church, to meet guests as they arrive at the sanctuary doors, and to lead guests down the aisle to be seated. In a traditional wedding, the bride's family and friends are seated on one side and the groom's on the other. However, it is good if you ask the couple in advance if one side of the new family is likely to have a lot more guests than the other. There are many good reasons why one family may be present *en masse* while the other is less represented, and it is good to be sensitive to this so there won't be any unnecessary embarrassment. If one side has a much larger contingent than the other (or even if not), the couple may prefer that the two families be mingled throughout.

■ seating immediate family members

MOTHERS & STEPMOTHERS

Traditionally, everyone except the bridal party is seated before the mothers enter. An usher escorts the groom's mother in and seats her, and then the bride's mother is escorted in last. When she is seated, this is the unspoken signal to all that the wedding service is about to begin. (One reason a mother might not enter at this time and in this manner would be if she is walking her daughter the bride down the aisle or if she is entering with her son, the groom.)

In any number of circumstances, these "mothers" may, indeed, not be actual mothers, but each one represents the primary female nurturer in each family. Seating them after everyone else is seated is a sign of honor.

If the mother of the bride is now married to someone other than the father, she will still have the priority seat (first row), but her current husband will have been ushered in alone and will already be there when she arrives. If she is single, she may sit alone or with other children or a family member of her choice who has been seated in advance of her.

FATHERS & STEPFATHERS

The father of the groom will usually come down the aisle just slightly behind his wife, and will join her once she is seated.

However, if the mother of the groom is no longer his wife, it is best that the father (and his current partner) be seated along with the rest of the guests, usually in the second row or not too far back.

In traditional weddings, the father of the bride has the honor of bringing his beautiful daughter (as all brides we know are beautiful) down the aisle to meet her groom. Today, the bride's mother may join them (more on that later, as well). The bride's father will then sit with his wife, the bride's mother, as soon as the words of the "giving of the bride" have been spoken.

However, if he is now married to someone other than the bride's mother, he will go to sit alongside his already-seated wife. If he and the bride's mother are divorced but both are currently single, then each should be asked separately and in advance whether they wish to sit together. If they decide not to sit together, then the mother will be seated in the front pew and the father close by, where and with whom he chooses. Remember, these are the kinds of issues that you, as the pastor, can deal with in advance, to facilitate a good experience for all concerned.

GRANDPARENTS & GREATGRANDPARENTS

These relatives will usually sit close to the parents, in the same row or one row behind. They are often escorted to their seats just before the mothers. Depending on their age and physical condition, they may need to be as close as possible to see or hear the proceedings well. Preparations for their comfort—such as cushioned seating or someone to assist them in and out of the sanctuary—should obviously be made in advance, especially if they are in wheelchairs and your church is not handicapped accessible.

SIBLINGS NOT IN THE WEDDING PARTY

In many circumstances, sisters and brothers are not in the wedding party. They are usually seated in the second row from the front, with each other and with their spouses and children, if they have them. Siblings are sometimes needed to assist with an elder family member or with other children.

CHILDREN IN THE FAMILY

Children who are the siblings of the bride or groom, or who belong to the bridal couple, should be seated up front with their families. It is good for children to be seated in a place where they can see and hear the proceedings. But it is also good for families with small children to be seated where they can get out quickly (at the ends of pews) if it becomes necessary to take restless children to the narthex or outside the church to give them a chance to settle down. (They can be brought back in as soon as they are ready.) It is absolutely unfair to the bridal couple, who will only have this one time (we hope) to be married, to have their wedding marred by crying or noisy children.

THEOLOGICAL REFLECTION

Then he took a little child and he put it among them; and taking it in his arms, he said to them, "Whoever welcomes one such child in my name welcomes me, and whoever welcomes me welcomes not me but the one who sent me." —Mark 9:36–37

Children were important to Jesus. He not only welcomed them, but he made it clear that if we welcome the little ones, the vulnerable, the helpless, we are welcoming Jesus himself.

■ seating very special guests

Be sure the couple tells you what special guests they are expecting, such as a family from out of town, very dear old friends, or people of particular distinction who deserve some special attention. Be sure the ushers are informed and know where these guests might be seated. Here are a few examples:

SOMEONE WHO SERVED AS A PARENT

In many cases, this person(s) should be seated wherever the parent would normally sit. If the birth parent is taking that role for the wedding, then the beloved person who served as a parent for the bride or groom will need to be seated fairly close by, in a place of honor.

OUT-OF-TOWN GUESTS WHO HAVE TRAVELED A DISTANCE

If guests have traveled a long way to attend, the couple may want to honor their efforts by having them seated behind the immediate family.

AN ACTIVE OR RECENT MEMBER OF THE MILITARY

All those present will want to show respect and gratefulness for the willingness of this person to serve our country in a difficult and dangerous time. For this reason he or she might be seated immediately behind the family members (or with the family, if part of the family). Since, in military weddings, people are seated according to rank, if a number of military people are attending the wedding, ask one of them to explain to you and the ushers how they are to be seated.

VISITING CLERGY, EVEN IF THEY ARE NOT "ON DUTY"

Clergy are often invited to be seated up front, especially in the African American community. This may not be the tradition of your church, but if it is the tradition of the clergy person who is visiting, or of either side of the bridal family, it is a welcoming gesture and will be appreciated.

A DIGNITARY

Who constitutes a dignitary varies widely from one community to another, but the general rule is that if the families view the person as a dignitary, then he or she is one! These guests should be given special seating wherever the family would like them to be placed, at both the church and the reception.

A CELEBRITY OR SOMEONE "FAMOUS"

It is unlikely, at the average wedding, that a celebrity or "famous" person will be attending, but it does happen. The bridal couple will surely tell you in advance all about this person's coming. If the celebrity can be seated where he or she can be seen by all, without a big production being made of it, then everyone who was expecting to see that person will be satisfied. On the other hand, the celebrity may specifically request to be seated at the rear of the sanctuary so as not to distract attention from the bride and groom, or because the celebrity prefers the privacy of that space. There will always be time later for any needed focus on that person. Today the stars are, of course, the bride and groom.

 **processional options**

■ "here comes the bride": new configurations

As the famous chorus from Wagner's *Lohengrin* (in its English translation) says, "Here Comes the Bride." This is the culmination of the procession. But *who* is in the processional and in *what order* they come down the aisle will vary, depending on the bride or groom's wishes. Traditionally, the men (groom, best man, and groomsmen) will walk in with the pastor from the side, immediately after the seating of the mothers. Following this, the bridal entrance music starts and the women enter from the back of the sanctuary. But in today's ceremonies, there are as many options as there are people involved. There are no hard-and-fast rules for the "correct order" of the processional. Generally, a procession will start with bridesmaids, then the flower girl and/or ring bearer, followed by the maid or matron of honor immediately before the bride and those who accompany her.

JUNIOR BRIDESMAIDS & YOUNG ATTENDANTS/USHERS

Those chosen to be junior bridesmaids and young attendants are usually in their preteens or early teen years, which, we all know, is a vulnerable age. It's a time when young people often feel uncomfortable in their growing bodies and are also painfully shy. Yet, as embarrassed as they may seem, it is likely that these kids will also be secretly deeply moved and honored to have been asked to serve in a wedding party. The wedding will very likely remain strong and clear in their memories for the rest of their lives.

As pastor, you can help make these young people more comfortable. Be sure they clearly understand the directions they have been given and help them relax in their role in the wedding. If you have a chance before the wedding, chat with them a bit as young adults rather than children. They are sure to appreciate your consideration.

BRIDESMAIDS, GROOMSMEN & USHERS

THEOLOGICAL REFLECTION

Then the kingdom of heaven will be like this. Ten bridesmaids took their lamps and went to meet the bridegroom. Five of them were foolish, and five were wise.—Matthew 25:1–2

The "bridesmaids" parable of Jesus is, of course, not directly about weddings or bridesmaids. Still, the story sheds a bit of light on at least some weddings at the time of Jesus. We may be surprised that a first-century Jewish wedding might have as many as ten bridesmaids. We may not be surprised that five are called wise and five foolish. The friends whom today's couples choose to stand with them on their day will not be perfect. They may be wise. They may be foolish. But they have been chosen, and we pastors need to respect that choice.

Bridesmaids come in all ages, sizes, and personalities. As mentioned earlier, some brides seem to choose them for their beauty or height in order to make a "pretty set" for the wedding photos. Others choose beloved siblings and friends without consideration of these matters. These bridal photos surely have their own kind of beauty and symmetry.

It's good to keep in mind that nothing is set in stone when it comes to processionals. For example, the groomsmen may be matched up with the bridesmaids and asked to walk down the aisle, rather than stand waiting at the front of the church with the groom.

It's also good to remember that many bridesmaids, as well as groomsmen, get a bit nervous before the wedding. If you ask what concerns them, they'll often tell you that they're worried about making a mistake, or not walking at the correct pace down the aisle, or not remembering how or with whom to make the entrance or the exit. If people are feeling anxious, you can usually see it in their faces. Your words of assurance as pastor can go a long way toward calming them. Remind them that they have rehearsed each step and reassure them that you expect things will go smoothly.

FLOWER GIRLS & RING BEARERS

How wonderful are the children in every wedding party! But children get nervous, too, and they tend to get tired or feel shy more quickly than the rest of us. Depending on their age, they often become apprehensive when they begin to sense the mood of others and intuitively become aware of the solemnity of the wedding. There is something about getting all dressed up and then walking down an aisle with everyone staring at you, however lovingly, that can be disconcerting to someone under ten!

Being suddenly struck with terror and stopping in their tracks is a common problem for younger flower girls/ring bearers. The way to avoid it is never—I mean *never*—plan for a little child to go down the aisle first! If children are more or less in the middle of the processional, they are much less likely to balk or panic.

But it's also good to have a back-up plan. If a child stops, a bridesmaid can take the hand of the child and either carry or walk alongside the child; or a parent or someone with whom the child feels safe can lovingly take the child out of the processional and have the child sit with them. Everyone understands that a child does not always wish to be choreographed to adult plans. Whether the child is actually "up there" with the bridal party or not, all will see how beautiful and sweet the child is, and the child will probably be willing and happy to return to the bridal party at some later point in the ceremony—or at least in time for the photos.

As pastor, your support of and encouragement for the little ones are just as important as they are for anyone else in the bridal party. In addition, their adult family members and the bridal couple will really appreciate any kindness you show toward these children whom they have chosen to participate because they love them.

FLOWER GIRLS

Flower girls usually vary in age from three to ten and may be given a variety of little tasks. It is common for the bride to request that the flower girl walk immediately ahead of her down the aisle to strew flower petals from a small basket. There is no reason not to agree to this as, the truth be told, children nearly always forget to actually drop the petals! If they do strew the petals as they walk, there are usually not so many petals that the carpet would be damaged. Still, you might tell them not to drop too many, so the person walking after them won't slip on them and fall.

RING BEARERS

Ring bearers are usually little boys also from age three to ten, and they often process down the aisle with a small pillow that holds wedding rings. It is a very good idea that the actual wedding rings *not* be on that pillow but, rather, be in the care of the best man and/or maid or matron of honor. On too many occasions the real rings are either tied too tight or too loosely to ribbons on the pillow. If too tight, someone has to fight with the knots to get them undone when the time comes for the rings to be exchanged. If too loose, the rings have been known to come undone, roll to the floor, and sometimes even disappear under the pews! The best plan is to have two nice little dimestore-type rings tied on the pillow for "looks." This way, even if the young ring bearer decides to run to his mother with the pillow instead of staying in the bridal procession, the wedding will be able to go on, ring exchange and all.

SCENARIO

An adorable little two-and-a-half-year-old boy was to be ring bearer at the wedding of a rather young couple. During the rehearsal, as they were practicing the processional, the sweet little boy started off all right. But when he got about halfway down the aisle, he must have suddenly realized everyone was looking at him. He became terrified and stopped dead in his tracks. The pastor, who had only just met the bridal couple for a couple of sessions, turned to the bride, smiled warmly, and suggested, "If this happens tomorrow, let's just get his mother to come over and take him back with her to her seat."

The bride had a strange look on her face and then whispered to the pastor, "Actually, I am his mother. He thinks that my mother is his mother, but I'll get my mother to come and get him if this happens. Would that be okay?"

The surprised pastor said it would certainly be just fine. Bride was mother. Mother was grandmother. The pastor never did find out whether the groom knew any of this. Another wedding! They are all different!

PEOPLE "OF HONOR":
MAID OR MATRON OF HONOR, BEST MAN

Most brides and grooms have a sibling or special friend whom they ask to be the maid (single) or matron (married) of honor and the best man. These roles are truly an honor for those who are invited, but they are also a responsibility. It is up to these chosen dear ones to do everything in their power to see that the couple's special day is a success. But, of course, not everything is within their power! They can only help and support. Still, these are the people you as the pastor might go to if you need assistance in areas related to the couple.

In today's world you may be surprised to find that the bride's best friend is a male or the groom's best pal is a woman. The couple may want these people to stand up with them at their wedding. Although such a configuration may come as a surprise to the wedding guests, it can be touching and meaningful if handled with grace. As long as the couple is comfortable and happy with their choices of attendants, there is no reason why you or anyone should push them into a wedding party with more traditional roles. Some of the titles listed in the wedding program may have to be changed, of course. You might use terms such as "bride's friend of honor" and "groom's friend of honor." The couple may already have decided on some appropriate terminology for those who serve in these capacities. Or you could say in the program something like this: "Standing up today with Mary is her dear friend Keith" or "Standing up today with John is his long-time friend Linda." As you help the couple plan the wedding, be sure that any who are taking these less traditional roles are also comfortable with them. If they are comfortable, then others at the wedding will be as well.

◼ who takes the bride down the aisle?

THEOLOGICAL REFLECTION
Therefore a man leaves his father and his mother and clings to his wife, and they become one flesh.—Genesis 2:24

At traditional weddings, it is the woman who kisses her father, is given away by her parents, and moves forward to begin a new life with her husband. Still, the ancient biblical writer of Genesis appears to have assumed the opposite; that it was the male of the couple who needed to move forward, emotionally at least, from his family of origin into the new family unit of himself and his spouse.

A wedding marks the official pronouncements and blessings that create a new family unit. This does not imply that the families of origin do not continue to be loved and respected. Still, in order to give the new family a chance to live and thrive, both bride and groom must be willing to move forward out of one family and into the new one.

Needless to say, the bride's father is the traditional choice to escort her down the aisle. But in our contemporary times, there are certainly other options. Today the choice is just as likely to be both parents, a sibling or siblings, a child or children (young or adult) of either the bride or the groom, or even a very special or long-time family friend. Or the couple may wish to process down the aisle together, simply walking in hand-in-hand. Or the bride may choose to walk down the aisle on her own. Or the processional may not happen at all! The couple may choose to enter separately but simultaneously, with or without family, from opposite sides of the sanctuary, meeting at the center. This can create a very beautiful and strong image of two equal partners choosing to share their lives.[1] Here are some options you can offer the couple:

A FATHER OR FATHER-FIGURE

If the father is to escort the bride, this works out nicely for the dad because it gives him an opportunity to spend those few but very special moments with his beloved daughter, after the music has begun and before they start that walk down the aisle that will change her life forever. Most people never get to witness the joy and intimacy of these moments. As the pastor, however, when you look their way to see if they are ready to begin the processional, you may catch a glance. Priceless! These touching and often wordless moments surely solidify a bond between father and daughter in a time that the father is probably feeling somewhat vulnerable. Does he really want to "give away" his little girl to this man, however fine that man may be? With or without words, his daughter assures him that this is what she wants, and his walking her down the aisle then is representative of his blessing of the marriage.

A MOTHER OR MOTHER-FIGURE

There is no reason why a mother cannot assume this traditional role and escort her daughter down the aisle. Especially in a case where the bride does not have a father, she might choose her mom to walk with her and speak the words of giving, as the mother presents her daughter to be married.

BOTH PARENTS

It is not uncommon today for a bride to be escorted down the aisle by both parents. This works best if the aisle is actually wide enough to accommodate three! Still, it can probably be accomplished in any church aisle by walking closely together. Just be sure that the width of the skirt of the wedding gown is taken into consideration. It is quite beautiful for everyone at the wedding to see the three entering the sanctuary arm-in-arm. There is a visual sense of the bride being enfolded on both sides by the love and warmth of family.

A SIBLING OR SIBLINGS

The bride might also choose a sister or brother to walk with her down the aisle. In particular, if the father has passed away or is unable to attend for any reason, the bride might ask her brother. Most brothers and sisters who are asked to take this honored role in the wedding are deeply moved.

THE BRIDE'S CHILD/REN

It is particularly poignant when a woman about to be married chooses to ask her own child (whether a small child, youth, or adult) to walk her down the aisle. The son or daughter, in most cases, is pleased and proud. The acceptance of this task is also a symbol that the child of the bride is approving of the new marriage relationship. By taking the bride down the aisle, he or she is, in essence, bestowing a blessing that greatly helps the newly formed family get a good start.

OTHER CLOSE FAMILY OR FRIEND(S)

Some brides, for a variety of reasons, do not have any family members who can walk them down the aisle. She might choose to ask a close friend, either male or female, to do the honors. Or she may choose to walk down the aisle alone or with her groom.

▇ who, if anyone, "gives this woman"?

It needs to be emphasized here that there is absolutely no reason whatsoever why any bride in the twenty-first century should have to be "given away" to the man she will marry. It is fully evident in our culture and to everyone concerned that the woman is a free agent, and that she and the groom are choosing to join into an equal, mutual, loving, and permanent relationship.

A couple might do the "giving" of themselves freely to each other. It is also appropriate for the families of both the bride and groom to "give" their offspring. However, for many brides it is still traditional for the person or persons who walk her down the aisle to "give" her to be married. The chosen person stands with the bride, speaks the words of giving, kisses the bride (optional), and then moves back a step or two as the groom steps forward, takes the bride by the arm and, together, they move to stand before the pastor. This physical movement, along with the spoken words, is representative of the bride's move from her family of origin into the new family.

BY FATHER(S)

Fathers are still the traditional persons to "give" the bride, but their options for the actual words of the "giving" response are many. A father may say the old-fashioned "I do" or the more popular "her mother and I." (Even if he and her mother are divorced, this is still appropriate.) Or the father may include other family members in the response.

At one recent wedding, everyone was deeply touched when a father responded with words that included not only himself and his wife but the bride's two sisters and the grandparents who had passed away. Suddenly the room seemed filled with the presence of the entire family, everyone who had cared for and nurtured this lovely bride, both those present that day and those beyond. It was a beautiful moment.

BY MOTHER(S)

It is certainly possible for the mother or a representative of the mother to "give" the bride. She may say, "I do," or if there is a father, she may say, "Her father and I."

BY BOTH PARENTS/STEPPARENTS, SIBLINGS, OR CHILDREN

These people might respond by simply saying, "We do," or they may have a suggestion of their own. If it seems appropriate, do let them. You might even want to add a particularly good response to your own repertoire of suggestions when a similar situation presents itself.

$\mathcal{8}$ unity candles & communion

THEOLOGICAL REFLECTION

You are the light of the world. A city built on a hill cannot be hid. No one af-ter lighting a lamp puts it under the bushel basket, but on the lampstand, and it gives light to all in the house. In the same way, let your light shine before others, so that they may see your good works, and give glory to your Father in heaven.—Matthew 5:14–16

The metaphor of light has always been popular and beautiful. Even after many decades of electric light (per-haps even more so today *because* of electric light), we continue to be deeply moved by the sight of a simple, lit candle. Its flickering flame and its gentle glow symbolize that light eliminates darkness and illuminates all that is pure and beautiful. The light that shines from a unity can-dle in a wedding ceremony can bring to mind the very glory of God's creation: "Then God said, 'Let there be light'; and there was light. And God saw that the light was good" (Genesis 1:3–4a).

■ some thoughtful considerations for unity candles

The usual arrangement for unity candles is one central candle with one slim candle on either side. Most often the two outside candles are already lit when the service begins. When the time co-mes for the lighting of the center candle, the couple each takes one of the lit candles and, together, lights the middle candle. Follow-ing this, it used to be traditional for them to blow out the single candles and place them back in their holders.

The trouble with blowing out their individual candles is the symbolic implication that they are giving up their individual iden-tities. It seems more appropriate that each take a lit candle, to-gether light the center candle that represents their being "as one," and then place their individual candles back in the holders *still lit*. (This may vary according to the theological stance of the couple and of the church.)

◼ some practical considerations

There are also some practical matters to consider with unity candles. Some special care is needed on your part to monitor this portion of the service, to give clear directions to the couple, and to rehearse it well so that all will go smoothly.

POSITION

The unity candles need to be in a good central spot. The altar or communion table is not usually the best place for them. They would be better on a special small but stable stand or table, behind the altar or communion table, or to the side.

SAFETY

Someone needs to make sure that the candles are securely attached, but that the outside candles are easy to remove (for the lighting of the central candle) and easy to put safely back in place. A number of things can go wrong, some of which are related to the mix of bridal veils and fire! When the bride is wearing clothing she is unaccustomed to wearing and moving in a small unfamiliar space, and possibly being somewhat nervous, caution is in order.

THE BRIDE'S GOWN

In most situations, the groom will turn to the bride, take her arm, and escort her a short distance to where the unity candles are located. She will need to give her bridal bouquet to her first attendant, if this has not already been done. Also, if she is wearing a long gown, she may have to gently kick it around with her foot so that it is in the right direction for her short walk. Then, when returning, she will have to kick it again. Otherwise, she may find her gown wound around her legs, leaving her almost trapped. (Today there are fewer and fewer women accustomed to wearing long, flowing gowns, so this tip may be greatly appreciated.) Another possibility is that the attending maid or matron may follow behind the bride and adjust the bottom and the direction of the gown as needed.

SPECIAL MUSIC

You might want to suggest to the couple that this time of the lighting of the unity candle is an appropriate opportunity for additional special music.

■ some options for lighting

BY THE MOTHER OF THE BRIDE & MOTHER OF THE GROOM (OR REPRESENTATIVES)

Often, the groom's mother and the bride's mother go up together and light the two individual candles just before the official service begins. It can be very beautiful symbolically for the gathered congregation to see the two mothers together. However, they should do this only if both feel comfortable in doing so.

BY THE BRIDE, GROOM, & THEIR CHILDREN

Sometimes children of either the bride or the groom participate in the lighting of candles. In these situations, encourage the couple to put together their own style of unity candles, possibly with one taper to represent each child as well as themselves. Before the lighting of the candles, you can explain how the candles represent this new family bonding.

■ communion options

THEOLOGICAL REFLECTION

For I received from the Lord what I also handed on to you, that the Lord Jesus on the night when he was betrayed took a loaf of bread, and when he had given thanks, he broke it and said, "This is my body that is for you. Do this in remembrance of me." In the same way he took the cup also, after supper, saying, "This cup is the new covenant in my blood. Do this, as often as you drink it, in remembrance of me." For as often as you eat this bread and drink the cup, you proclaim the Lord's death until he comes.
—I Corinthians 11:23–26

To receive communion means different things to different people. For many, communion is the receiving of the body and blood of Christ for forgiveness, for receiving Christ's presence, and love. For others, communion is symbolic of a shared meal in which the people who are partaking in the act of the eating and drinking together become the body of Christ. In whatever way the act of communion is understood, it will always be a communing with and remembrance of Jesus Christ.

In some churches, the bridal couple will have the option to include communion, the Lord's Supper, as part of the wedding service. It is more common for communion to be served in an orthodox wedding than, for example, in a Free Church wedding. This is partly because, in the orthodox churches (Roman Catholic, Eastern Orthodox, Anglican/ Episcopalian, and Lutheran) communion is part of most worship services. In a Free Church, communion might be served only four to six times a year and would be optional at a wedding. In a Free Church, also, emphasis would be placed on the fact that the people communing would be members of the gathered community, and every member of the church would be invited and expected to be present.

Because weddings are events to which we invite people we care about from all areas of our lives, the result is that there are likely to be people from many faith traditions—or of no faith at all. To offer communion could put these people in very uncomfortable positions, especially if your denomination welcomes only church members to the table. Or in the case of open communion, even with a warm invitation from you to participate, some may feel a sense of discomfort because they are not familiar with your church's way of serving and receiving communion.

However, if the couple is determined to include communion, the sharing of communion can certainly enhance the sense of worship for the couple and for the guests, and the sharing of bread and cup can also serve to build community. Encourage the couple to include an appropriate invitation in the wedding program, with clear instructions as to how the juice/wine and bread are to be taken and shared. There are many different ways that you might serve the elements. Congregants may come forward and receive them from the pastor—even from the bride and groom, in some denominations, if they are both members of the church. Bread and small cups may be passed from person to person. (The passing of the elements is often the work of the church's deacons. If so, they might be invited to the wedding and given this task.) If you are relatively new as pastor of the church, it is best to check with your deacons or elders before agreeing to include communion in the wedding.

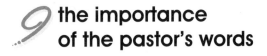

the importance of the pastor's words

helping everyone feel welcome

THEOLOGICAL REFLECTION
Young men and women alike, old and young together! Let them praise the name of the Lord.—Psalm 148:12–13a

The wedding service is always a service of worship and, in most cases, a gathering of "young" and "old." We're reminded in Psalm 148 (and in numerous other places in scripture) that all generations of people are called to praise God. Weddings are important to children, and most of them will long remember their participation. For older people, weddings bring memories of weddings past, and are also proof that life and love continue from generation to generation. It is important that everyone feel welcome.

The words you as pastor use in welcoming everyone to the service can go a long way toward helping every person in the wedding party and everyone attending the wedding feel comfortable and at ease. Remind people that they are valued by God and that they are warmly and openly welcomed in this worship place, whatever their race, age, faith background, or socioeconomic level. As an example, you might say something like this:

On behalf of myself and the entire congregation, I extend to you a warm welcome to this church. Let us remember, as we

celebrate together the joyous occasion of this wedding, that
God loves every one of us of every age, from the youngest to
the oldest, more than we can ever know!

As the wedding ceremony progresses, it is nice if you can give
the gathered guests the opportunity to respond in some way by offering their blessing on the marriage, along with a promise of their
continuing support of the couple in the vows they have made to
each other. An easy way to include this is simply to ask the wedding guests to respond to your words with "we do." Or you might
ask everyone to repeat together some words printed in the program. This way, every person at the wedding is truly included and
has a chance to participate.

I want to add one note of caution, however. Some pastors
have been known to engage wedding guests at a level that can be
uncomfortable for some. As an example, at one wedding a pastor
asked every married couple to turn to each other and renew their
marriage vows. A ripple of discomfort ran through the crowd, but
the pastor proceeded unaware! The fact is, any decent-sized gathering of people will inevitably include some couples who are happily married and some who are less so. It is unfair to coerce
couples, most of whom you do not know, to renew their vows in a
public gathering. The decision to renew vows is very personal.
Also, this wedding is about the couple getting married, and the
focus needs to stay on them.

▓ delivering wedding sermons that include everyone

Even though the sermon or meditation you deliver as pastor is
presented intimately to the couple and relates to the couple's relationship with God and each other and the days and years ahead, it
is also (over)heard by everyone present. Your message can be
meaningful to the others as well, especially if what you say includes, even if very subtly, the fact that God loves us all; that we
are always invited to know God better; that we are called to love
each other and to be people of hope, just as this couple is on this
special day.

As pastors, we also need in some way to remind the couple—and every person present—that, even though all of us make

mistakes, there is forgiveness; that, even though life can bring suffering, God is always with us and for us. For those who are not accustomed to attending church, these reassurances are a way to draw them toward God without being demanding or threatening. (See Part Three for suggestions for biblical passages and wedding sermons.)

◼ helping the couple with appropriate exchanges

EXCHANGING VOWS

THEOLOGICAL REFLECTION

"Blessed are you, O God of our Ancestors, and blessed is your name in all generations forever. You made Adam, and for him you made his wife Eve as a helper and support. From the two of them the human race has sprung. You have said, 'It is not good that a man should be alone; Let us make a helper for him like himself.' I am now taking this kinswoman of mine, not because of lust, but with sincerity. Grant that she and I may find mercy and that we may grow old together." And they both said, "Amen, Amen."
—Tobit 8:4–8

Few passages in the Bible relate directly to weddings, and none to wedding vows. There is one little known passage, however, found among the extra books known by Protestants as the Apocrypha and by Roman Catholics as the Deutero-canonical books. This passage in Tobit offers a clear example of the Jewish covenantal perception of marriage. A young man named Tobit, for whom the book is titled, binds himself to young Sarah. Her parents have given their blessing and now they are alone. Although Tobit's prayer is not a vow spoken directly to the bride, his words speak his good intentions and his promises to Sarah in a form somewhat parallel to our contemporary wedding vows of "for better or for worse, till death do us part." Sarah's joining him in the "Amen, Amen" represents her vow, in return, to her new husband.

Many people dream (or read in popular wedding books) of creating, memorizing, and then speaking their own vows to each other on the great day. Though this may be the ideal, it is seldom advisable. Not only can the preparation of memorized vows be terribly time consuming and distracting, but it can also interfere with the couple's enjoyment of the wedding itself. Brides and grooms may be beautiful people, but they are not usually professional performers. In the excitement and intense emotions of the day, they may completely forget their memorized vows. Even in the best of situations, the bride or groom is likely to be nervous about remembering the vows instead of truly being able to enjoy the preparations for the wedding and the wedding itself.

SCENARIO

The bride and groom had written their own vows. Early in the ceremony, however, the bride wept so many tears of joy on the paper on which her vows had been written that, when the moment came, her words were no longer legible. She tried to come up with something ad lib and then desperately looked at the pastor, who had the presence of mind to proceed with the traditional wedding vows. Later at the reception someone came up to the pastor and said, "I loved the service, but what were the bride and groom doing with those pieces of paper they were holding?" The pastor thought up all kinds of good answers but, remembering his ordination vows to always tell the truth in love, his answer was this: "It's always good to give them a prop to keep their hands busy."

The bride and groom will enjoy the wedding and experience the presence of God and their new relationship much more if they're not distracted by trying to recite memorized words. For this reason, I strongly recommend that you advise couples to repeat after you either traditional vows or vows that you have agreed upon together. There are a wide variety of options to choose from and many suggestions available on the Internet. At the time of this writing, these sites offered some good options:

www.myweddingvows.com
www.elegantvows.com
www.foreverwed.com/Religious_Ceremonies/
www.documentsanddesigns.com/wedding_vows.htm

If the two do write their own vows, be careful that they are promising what is required in Christian marriage. An example would be *not* to say "as long as we both shall *love*" but, rather, "as long as we both shall *live*." While our society's high divorce rate suggests that things may not turn out this way, still, a marriage that lasts a lifetime is at least the intent.

EXCHANGING RINGS

As already mentioned, it is better if the ring bearer is not carrying the real rings. Normally, it works well if the best man carries both the groom's and the bride's rings in a convenient jacket pocket. The maid or matron of honor could carry one ring, but she is highly unlikely to have a pocket in her bridesmaid's gown. Besides, she will be holding not only her own bouquet and, but also, during the service, the bride's flowers as well. And she is also expected to be ready to adjust the bride's gown if needed. Her hands will be full.

SCENARIO

A bride and groom had both been involved with raising and riding horses all of their lives. They loved horses, and they were buying a ranch in the Midwest. The bride called and announced to the pastor that the groom had expressed the desire to give her a horse in lieu of a wedding ring. She wanted to know if this was acceptable. What was the pastor to say?

In a way, it was not the pastor's business. The pastor explained, however, that, as touching as the idea of a horse might be, perhaps the horse would be better as a wedding gift from the groom than as the symbol in lieu of a wedding ring. After all, the pastor explained, a horse would die one day, very likely during the course of the marriage. Further, a simple gold band was not expensive and might serve as a better symbol of the unending love they shared. On the other hand, an actual ring wasn't technically needed for a wedding to take place. In this case, the couple took the pastor's advice.

EXCHANGING GIFTS

Gifts from the family and the guests to the bridal couple are a part of most weddings. In addition, a bride and groom sometimes want to exchange gifts within the context of the wedding ceremony. If the gifts are symbolic or they are items that are being passed on from generation to generation, then it might be very appropriate for the exchange to take place during the service. If, for example, a wedding ring has been in the family for years or generations, you could mention this at the beginning of your words about the significance of rings.

When children are becoming part of a new family unit that is being created by this marriage, the bride or groom may want to give them each a gift. Although the choice of the gift belongs to the bride or groom, you, as pastor, might confirm whether a specific gift would be appropriate. Every family is different. Still, for example, for the groom to give a ring to the bride's young daughter would not be such a good idea because the primary bond between the bride and groom is being symbolized by the rings they exchange. The young daughter's bonding with the new family might be better symbolized by the gift of a necklace or bracelet. You might also want to suggest that a symbolic gift, such as a handwritten scroll, a flower, a small book, or a Bible, can be just as important as a gift that costs a lot of money.

"I now pronounce you . . .": options for the declaration

THEOLOGICAL REFLECTION

[Jesus said] "For this reason a man shall leave his father and mother and be joined to his wife, and the two shall become one flesh. So they are no

longer two, but one flesh. Therefore what God has joined together, let no one separate."—Mark 10:7–9

In this passage, Jesus is not just saying that couples are obliged to stay together but that, in some mysterious way, God has made them one. Why so many divorces today, we might ask? Is it because people do not take their vows seriously? Perhaps so. But there are also couples whom, it appears, God truly does bind together in ways that no one can separate. As we officiate at each wedding, it is our hope that the couple who stands before us is, indeed, one of those blessed couples who will truly become "one flesh."

The culmination of the wedding is the moment when you, the pastor, declare that the couple is officially married, that they are now husband and wife. Then it is your job to present the now-married couple to the gathered congregation. Traditionally, pastors have said, "Ladies and gentlemen, I now present to you Mr. and Mrs. John Smith." These days, however, there are a variety of choices of wording. It is common now for the woman not to change her name at marriage. In these cases, the pastor can offer options at the time of the planning of the wedding, something along these lines:

> *"Ladies and gentlemen, I present to you John Smith and Mary Jones, husband and wife."*

> *"Ladies and gentlemen, I present to you the newest married couple: Mary Jones and John Smith."*

The couple may have another way they would like to be announced—as spouses, partners, or with other titles. Be sure to ask them what they prefer.

■ "you may kiss the bride"

THEOLOGICAL REFLECTION
While he [Jacob] was still speaking with them Rachel came with her father's sheep; for she kept them. Now when Jacob saw Rachel . . . Jacob kissed Rachel and wept aloud.—Genesis 29:9–11

The biblical story of Rachel and Jacob appears to be an early example of love at first sight. Although Jacob ended up waiting years before he could make sweet Rachel his wife, eventually it did happen. The kiss and Jacob's tears were the sign of that love. Who of us is not touched by the joy of that moment? Today, couples nearly always seal their marriage vows with a kiss before God and the gathered witnesses.

Although the words "you may kiss the bride," or, in the case of true inclusivity, "you may kiss each other," or simply "you may kiss," are not required for the wedding ceremony to be sealed, this tradition continues as a loved and looked-for completion of the service. Be sure to ask the couple if they want the kiss to be included and find out what words they prefer you use for the invitation to kiss. *One practical note:* If the bride is wearing a veil, it may still be in place. The groom should lift the front of the veil that is covering her face and kiss her. The veil, by the way, should stay in its new position after the kiss. The occasional nervous groom has been known to place the veil back in front of the bride's face after the kiss. This action almost always causes giggles from the gathered guests and disturbs the seriousness of the mood.

10 expect the unexpected

◼ weeping

There is no guessing just who the weeper at the wedding might be! Traditionally, of course, it is the mother of the bride. There is generally no problem here. She simply needs to bring enough tissues or handkerchiefs to cover her needs. As long as her weeping is quiet, it is likely that most people will not even notice.

On the other hand, if it is the bride, the groom, or someone in the bridal party who weeps, the sounds, tears, and blowing noses are more likely to be public. It is a good idea for you as the pastor to be prepared. If you have a pocket in your robe or suit, tuck a few tissues in there. Sometimes tears of joy may even hold up the wedding vows. But people can wait, and everyone will understand and be touched. A little pat on the back or a bit of humor can help. Be sure, though, that your humor does not embarrass anyone.

■ fainting

Mostly, fainting at weddings happens only in the movies. Still, it could happen, and it's good to be prepared. The best idea is to prevent the fainting in the first place. There are a few clues to anticipating who might faint, although you can never be sure. Sometimes, a bridal party member will actually warn you at the rehearsal, saying, "I am afraid I'm going to faint at the wedding." Other times, you will see someone during the ceremony breathing in a very high and shallow manner, perspiring, or looking pale. If fainting is even mentioned in jest at the rehearsal (often, but not always, the bride), you might offer the following tips:

- Instead of worrying about whether you'll make a mistake, or what others might be thinking, try to concentrate on the words that are being spoken, remember how happy you are, and try to relax.
- Slow down your breathing, and breathe more deeply.
- Be sure your clothing is not too tight.
- Make sure you have enough to eat and drink (and do not drink alcohol) before the service. Wedding party members often get busy and involved and forget to eat on the wedding day. Get some protein in you before arriving at the church.

If a child in the wedding party is overly nervous or prone to pass out, it is best that some person in the wedding party or family be prepared to take the child out or, at the very least, stand close and hold onto him or her.

If someone actually does faint, simply stop the proceedings and tell everyone that we are going to take care of this first and then return for the rest of the wedding. Get the person seated and advise they put their head down between their knees for a few minutes. A sip of water will help, so it does not hurt to have one behind the pulpit or lectern. Some tissue back there is often handy as well, in case of a nosebleed or too many tears.

SCENARIO

Papa didn't approve of the man his beloved daughter was about to marry. Still, he had agreed to attend the wedding. Many family members and friends were more than a bit nervous about what Papa might do or say when the time came for the pastor to speak the words, "If anyone has just cause that these two may not be joined together, let him speak now or forever hold his peace." Would Papa shout out, "I object" or would he hold his peace? Might he grab his daughter, the bride, and drag her out of the church? He had been known to be excitable!

Just as the pastor was about to speak those words, the bride's little sister, the flower girl, began to faint to the floor. Papa ran down the aisle, picked up his precious younger daughter, and rushed her out into the fresh air. While they were outside the door, the pastor, wisely, went on with the ceremony. By the time Papa and the younger daughter returned, just minutes later, the two were already pronounced husband and wife. Little sister had recovered from her fainting spell, and the happy and relieved guests headed out to the reception to celebrate. Papa ended up being just fine and, in time, found his new son-in-law to be like a son.

■ surprises

Most wedding surprises will not be as dramatic as the above scenario. Nevertheless, as the pastor, it behooves us to be ready for the unexpected. Wedding days are dramatic days, no matter how calm the couple may seem to be. All you can do is try to keep things going as planned, adjust to the surprises, and, if absolutely necessary, stop the proceedings and help everyone to stay calm until the problem is solved. Whatever happens, everyone will be looking to you as the one at the helm.

Although it is rare, there is always the remote possibility that an ex-lover or ex-spouse may turn up and misbehave at the wedding. There is no way to plan for such an event. If the couple tells you that there is any possibility that someone might show up to disrupt the wedding, you might suggest that they arrange for a strong but very calm family member or friend to be prepared to encourage the person to leave the sanctuary or to escort the person out. It is vital, however, that the person being encouraged to leave is *not physically touched at all*, as this provides grounds for litigation. We all hope no such unexpected visitors will appear but, if they do, the first priority is, "Do not engage in arguments with them or attempt to physically remove them." Sometimes it may be better to just stop the proceedings for a few minutes and let the person speak his or her mind. The person is likely to leave once he or she has said her peace.

SCENARIO

George was a singer who agreed to get a musical group together to perform at a wedding. It was a huge wedding with over four hundred guests, in a large church. Everything went smoothly at first. The group performed, and the time came for the vows. When the pastor asked the groom, "Do you take this woman to be your wife?" his answer was the expected, "I do." But when the pastor asked the bride, "Do you take this man to be your husband?" there was total silence! And more silence.

Finally, the bride spoke. Standing there in her $1000-plus wedding gown, she slowly turned to the gathered congregation and said something like this: "Do I take this man to be my husband? I do not! Why not, you ask me? The answer is this. After promising to love me for a lifetime, this man was with my maid of honor, my best friend, last night, after he took me home from the rehearsal. Let the two of them live happily every after."

At this point, the beautiful weeping and very angry bride took off running up the aisle and out of the church. The musicians, the bridal party, and the gathered guests sat in stunned silence simply waiting, for about a half hour. Then they got up and went home. The bride's parents were the big losers. They had spent over

$20,000 on the wedding and the reception that never was.

George the singer was pleased that a week or so later he still received his check.

11 closing matters

◼ options for exits: the recessional

THE TRADITIONAL (HASTY) EXIT

Once the declaration has taken place and it is time for the bridal party to leave the sanctuary, most organists or pianists will know that the music is to become upbeat and joyful. (If not, with all due respect to the musician's musical expertise, you might suggest it.) In a traditional wedding, the couple will exit first, with the groom extending his arm to his bride, and the two walking out briskly together down the aisle with all the vigor that love and new hopes can bring. The couples in the bridal party will follow, usually in pairs, each groomsman meeting with one fair maiden, and any children simply following as it is their turn. You, the "parson," will take up the rear.

STOPPING ALONG THE WAY

A second option may be more family-friendly and is especially appropriate if the families are very close. In this version of the exit, the couple may stop en route and pick up a flower(s) from the altar or communion table. The bride may offer a flower and a kiss to her mother and a grandmother, if one is present, or to her mother and the groom's mother. Or the groom may kiss his mother, and the bride, her mother, before continuing the exit up the aisle. Any number of variations are possible, such as the groom giving a flower to his new wife's mother and the bride giving one to his mother. This kind of exit from the sanctuary has symbolic significance. It is a way of saying, "Yes, we are now a new family unit, but our love and respect for our families of origin is strong and continues on into our new family."

■ the marriage license

Now it's time to go home. You've counseled them. You've rehearsed them. You've married them. But wait just a minute! Not quite yet!

All through my ministry, I was sure I would make this one mistake: I would forget to mail in the signed marriage certificate. In all the flurry, especially right after you perform the ceremony, it would be so easy to forget. So, don't. Go right from the sanctuary back to your office, not allowing anything or anyone to stop you. Immediately pick up the marriage license/certificate (which you will have left out on your desk as visible as possible). Pick up a nice black-inked pen and sign the paper. I also suggest that you do not sign it until *after* you have performed the service, just in case the couple changed their minds at the last minute.

Then, take the license/certificate in one hand and the pen in the other and go directly to the best man and maid or matron of honor. Do not leave them until they have signed the document. Head back to your office, make a photocopy for your records if you wish, and place the original in a stamped envelope (again, which you have prepared in advance). Put it right beside your bag or coat so it will be a priority. When you leave, walk or drive directly to the nearest mailbox and drop it in.

Once this is done, you are free to go, and not before. The couple is not officially married if this signed document does not arrive at the appropriate government office on time. In some states you are even liable if you don't send it in.

By the way, I never actually forgot to mail one, but I sure came close more than once.

12 the wedding reception
(if you choose to attend)

THEOLOGICAL REFLECTION

On the third day there was a wedding in Cana of Galilee, and the mother of Jesus was there. Jesus and his disciples had also been invited to the wedding. When the wine gave out, the mother of Jesus said to him, "They have no wine." And Jesus said to her, "Woman, what concern is that to you and to me? My hour has not yet come." His mother said to the servants, "Do whatever he tells you." Now standing there were six stone water jars for the Jewish rites of purification, each holding twenty or thirty gallons. Jesus said to them, "'Fill the jars with water." And they filled them up to the brim. And he said to them, "Now draw some out, and take it to the chief steward." So they took it. When the steward tasted the water that had become wine, and did not know where it came from (though the servants who had drawn the water knew) the steward called the bridegroom and said to him, "Everyone serves the good wine first, and then the inferior wine after the guests have become drunk. But you have kept the good wine until now." Jesus did this, the first of his signs, in Cana of Galilee, and revealed his glory; and his disciples believed in him.—John 2:1–11

The Gospel of John describes a wedding reception that Jesus, his disciples, and his mother attended. From this story, which we understand as Jesus' first miracle, the making of the water into wine, we learn that Jesus is no ordinary person. The story also suggests that God desires us to recognize special moments in our lives and our relationships, and to celebrate them! Jesus made it possible, when the people themselves did not have the wherewithal to provide wine and plenty of it, to continue the celebration.

This story also gives some insight into what some weddings in Jesus' time might have been like. And they seem to have been quite grand affairs. The guests at this wedding seemed to be expecting wine, and a good deal of it. There were servants and a chief steward to take care of the guest's expectations. In this case it seems that the bridegroom was hosting the wedding. Today's wedding receptions may be hosted by the bride's parents (the traditional format), the groom's parents, parents of bride and groom sharing the expenses and organizing, or (more and more often) the couple themselves.

In many ways it would be theologically more appropriate for the congregation to host the meal that follows the wedding service because the bride and groom are becoming a new family in the church,[2] but this is rarely the case. The bottom line is that, no matter who hosts the party, it is a time for joy.

Just as with the rehearsal dinner, it is not required that you as pastor attend the wedding reception. Your decision will depend upon many factors. In many circumstances, once the service is over the pastor will simply return home. However, if you are the pastor of the bride, the groom, or if you expect to be the pastor of this new family, then it is likely that you will be invited with your spouse (if you have one) to attend the wedding reception. Your choice to accept will depend on a lot of factors: your schedule, whether you have to preach the next morning, how close you are to the bridal family or families, and sometimes even whether your presence will cause a financial burden on those paying for the wedding.

■ the grace-giver & why it might not be you

It was customary in years back for the pastor to be asked to offer a prayer of grace before the reception meal. This is less common today. It is entirely appropriate for the couple to choose some beloved family member to offer grace. Often, this gives the couple an opportunity to honor a person of their choice. Sometimes it is an elder of the family or a friend or family member who is clergy or retired clergy. Still, as the pastor, you will need to be prepared to offer the grace in case you are asked to do so.

■ why they seated you with whom & what is your job?

THEOLOGICAL REFLECTION
On one occasion when Jesus was going to the house of a leader of the Pharisees to eat a meal on the Sabbath, they were watching him closely . . .
When he noticed how the guests chose places of honor, he told them a par-

able. "When you are invited by someone to a wedding banquet, do not sit down at the place of honor, in case someone more distinguished than you has been invited by your host; and the host who invited both of you may come and say to you, 'Give this person your place,' and then in disgrace you would start to take the lowest place. But when you are invited, go and sit down at the lowest place, so that when your host comes, he may say to you, 'Friend, move up higher'; and then you will be honored in the presence of all who sit at the table with you. For all who exalt themselves will be humbled, and those who humble themselves will be exalted."
—Luke 14:1, 7–11

There you have it! Whenever I've attended wedding receptions, I have made it a little hobby to watch the pastors as they enter the room, and to see how well they might know or take seriously this passage. Some pastors, who assume their presence is an integral part of the celebration, proceed straight to the head table, assuming there will be a special place for them. Others hang back, demonstrating their admirable humility.

In recent years, pastors are included less and less as head-table guests, and head tables are not even the norm. This means that more and more of us have ended up sitting at the back of the banquet room for the entire evening, awaiting the call forward and often feeling more than a bit disgruntled. The advice of Jesus, nevertheless, is good and practical advice. It is others who will decide whether or not we pastors are to be honored, and not ourselves. In the larger picture, the parable reminds us that it is not only unseemly but ungodly to be vying for position.

Where, then, should you—and your spouse, if you have one—sit at the wedding reception? Most often tables are assigned to people in advance. Sometimes, although not often today, the pastor will be seated at some kind of head table or table near the head table, either as a sign of respect or in order to make it easier to give the prayer before the meal. Wherever you are seated, keep this in mind: If seating is assigned, you can assume that the family carefully chose the people they wanted to be with each other at each table.

Once the grace has been offered, you are free to relax and enjoy the festivities. Well, almost . . . It is always possible that you may have been seated with the "difficult" people of the family and friends, to help keep the peace. It may be that you have been placed at a table with all the "extras" who didn't seem to quite fit. Either way, the family is probably depending on you to help make that group congenial, so you are not exactly off the hook. Have a good time, but remember: In some respects, you are still "working."

SCENARIO

Lucy was excited about being maid of honor at the wedding of her best friend, Joan. Lucy had helped keep Joan calm when the water in the flower vase in the back seat of the car almost spilled all over their gowns. She'd managed to keep Joan calm when Aunt Sue and Uncle Joe arrived quite late for the wedding. She had even managed to help Joan stay calm when the organist forgot to play the favorite hymn they had arranged for so carefully and had clearly announced in the program. But when they arrived at the reception and walked in the door, the bride nearly lost it!

"Oh no," she cried out when she saw the head table. "I specifically ordered a champagne glass with a rose to be placed on top of my wedding cake. I've always despised those ridiculous little plastic bride and groom figures." Sure enough, there they were atop the cake: a little plastic bride and a little matching groom. It might not seem like an important thing, but it was to Joan, and it was her wedding day!

Lucy had to think fast. She sent the bride off to the ladies room to powder her nose, saying, "Don't worry about a thing. When you get back, everything will be all right." Lucy got to work. The room was still empty, as the guests had not arrived. She carefully pulled the little bride and groom off the cake and dropped them in a nearby garbage can. She found a champagne glass on the table, put in a bit of water, and placed it on top of the cake right where the little plastic figures had been. Now all she needed was the rose. With a small table knife, she carefully cut one small rose from her own bouquet and placed it in the glass. Just that minute, the bride returned, looked at the cake, and you could see her relax. Now it was her dream cake. Not a word was said about it, but the bride was happy. Sometimes it is the very little things that make all the difference. Lucy had been a good bridesmaid! She had put her mother's old saying "Necessity is the mother of invention" into very good practice.

■ the bridal party can often help

If you see that things are not going well for the bride and groom at the reception, it is not inappropriate for you to have a few words with someone in the wedding party who may be able to help. Of course, once the wedding service is over, if the reception is anywhere except at the church you serve, then you are only a guest. Still, you are their pastor for the day, if not permanently. If you can be helpful without being intrusive, you might be able to be of assistance. The maid of honor and the best man are usually the ones closest to the couple. You, along with them, may be able to step in if some intervention is needed.

* * *

Well, pastor, friend, colleague, now the wedding day is only a sweet memory—even for you. Pat yourself on the back. You'll sleep tonight. Or will you? You start thinking about it. There are a lot of weddings still ahead for you. What if you are asked to share the leadership of a wedding with the pastor down the street? What if a couple wants to be married in their backyard? What if your children or grandchildren want you to perform their wedding someday? Relax. Part Three will address these possibilities and many more.

part three

special circumstances

13 gay & lesbian weddings

■ a wedding is a wedding

A wedding is a wedding, and every wedding is beautiful and
unique. Gay and lesbian weddings are no exception. A marriage
and a wedding are, of course, not the same thing. A marriage is the
official joining together of two people who love each other and
who have already made a decision to face and live life together in
love and faithfulness for a lifetime. A wedding (at least, a church
or religious wedding) is the public event in which they make their
declarations before both Almighty God and human witnesses.

In July of 2005, the United Church of Christ, at its annual
Synod Assembly in Atlanta, Georgia, voted to give committed relationships between two men or two women its official blessing and
full approval. A number of individual states in the U.S. are engaged in decision making regarding full acceptance of gay and lesbian marriage, the right to marry being the legal right of every
citizen. The nations of Canada, The Netherlands, Spain, Belgium,
and South Africa have already ruled in favor of same-sex marriage.
It is likely that you, as a pastor, will be asked at some point to perform weddings for same-sex couples. It is also very possible that
you may have not performed such a wedding in the past, and the
issues addressed in this section may be helpful.

The first thing to do, especially if you are being asked for the first time, is to take a very honest look at yourself. If you find that you harbor any homophobic feelings, try to work them out. If you cannot, then find someone else to perform the wedding. It will be important for you to be with the couple, not against them. Also, if the service is to take place at the church you serve, be sure that your church's policies permit same-sex weddings. (If they do not, you will know best whether this is a good time to address the issue with your local congregation and denomination.) It may be that there are, as yet, no such policies in place in your church. If this is the case, it will be good for you, as pastor, to meet with your deacons or elders in advance of agreeing to perform the marriage.

The best strategy for the wedding preparation is to listen carefully to the desires, dreams, and plans of the couple. Then, if needed, make minor adjustments to your usual wedding service text so this can work for them in a way that is dignified and, as in every other wedding, in keeping with the sanctity of the occasion.

■ going down the aisle

In general, most gay or lesbian weddings will proceed just like any other wedding, but there are a few issues that need to be worked out in advance of the rehearsal. One of these is the matter of how the couple will enter the sanctuary as the service begins. In many cases, they will choose simply to walk in together, arm-in-arm. Or each partner might enter from a different direction, accompanied by a parent or parents, other family member, or close friend. There may be a traditional bridal procession with one member of the couple coming in with you to await the arrival of the partner who is in the procession. Or both could be in a longer processional, each coming on the arm of a family member. The couple will then meet in a central position, as any other couple, and come forward a few steps to face the pastor. If a family member accompanies each, then each person might be asked, "Who gives this person (named) to be married?" and the family member would respond, "I do", "We do," or, "His/her mother/father and I."

■ special significance of the exchange of rings

In the past, when legal marriage was not permitted between same sex couples, the exchange of rings, and especially the blessing of those rings by clergy, took on a very special significance for many gay and lesbian couples. Some of this profound importance of the rings as symbols of very real and enduring love has continued. Because a ring forms a continuing and unbroken circle, the symbol of the ring has given discriminated-against gay or lesbian persons a tangible reminder that their love for each other is like God's love, unending and unconditional. It is especially important that you, as the pastor, seek out and employ language of healing, blessing, hope, and love when you are praying over or blessing these rings, and when the couple places them on each other's fingers.

■ words of promise: the new "traditional" language

Some of the wedding service wording will need to be adjusted for a gay or lesbian wedding. Go over the words of your ceremony with a fine-toothed comb well in advance to avoid any gaffs. Substitute gender-neutral words wherever it is appropriate, using words such as "spouse," "partner," or "life partner" rather than "husband" or "wife." Be sure to ask the couple what words they currently use and prefer in this regard. New language will arise as more same-sex weddings are performed and liturgies are written. If you create new good language and liturgies, you might want to share these, or even have them published. They will be needed. (This new language may adapt itself to bring some new life to ceremonies for heterosexual couples as well!)

You can give the couple the option of repeating traditional vows or reading words they have written themselves. It may be even more significant for them, however, to repeat or respond to your reading of a version of the marriage vows that heterosexual couples have lovingly spoken to each other for so many years in the past:

> "I _____ take you _____ to be my lawfully wedded spouse/partner/mate, to have and to hold from this day forward, for better or for worse, for richer or for poorer, in sick-

ness and in health, to love and to cherish and, forsaking all others, keeping only unto you, as long as we both shall live."

As you would with any couple, it is important to stress, in both the counseling period and at the wedding, the importance of fidelity for a lifetime as part of the marriage commitment. Every couple needs to be reminded that, though no one can predict the future, they are making vows to face all of life together. We know that divorce happens—and it will with same-sex couples as it does with any other—still, the promises reflect their intentions that there be no separation between them. In the situation of same-sex couples, as with interfaith couples, they may face all kinds of unfairness and discrimination in the years ahead. Their commitment for a lifetime will be what sustains them. It is likely that the same-sex couple will already be wise and level-headed in this regard because of difficulties they have already come through.

◼ dealing with family members who do not yet understand

When you meet with the couple, get to know a bit about how family members are dealing with this new, permanent change in the family dynamic. If you are forewarned about anyone attending the wedding who might be uncomfortable about same-sex marriage, you will be more useful in that regard on the wedding day.

As a pastor, you will probably be surprised at the patience and grace with which the gay or lesbian couple handles those among their family and friends who are not ready to accept their marriage. Still, one or both of the marrying couple may be feeling particularly vulnerable on the day of the wedding, so it will be good if you can try to keep things on an even keel. These sexual identity issues are usually deeply felt, impossible to explain, and will not be resolved in a day—especially the day of the wedding. If the people who are troubled about the marriage have at least chosen to attend, the joy of the wedding day and the sincere love the couple demonstrates will certainly model to them that this relationship is about permanency, love, and commitment, just as their own relationships are.

One of the most difficult situations for a member of a gay or lesbian couple is when a parent or dearly loved relative says he or she might come and then does not show up at the wedding. You as pastor cannot stop the hurt, but you can remind the hurting member of the couple that this day is about them, their love, and their future, and that maybe the person is just not ready and will "come around" in time.

■ the special rewards of performing a gay or lesbian wedding

You may be nervous the first time you officiate at a gay or lesbian wedding, worrying about what others might think, whether you are doing the right thing, or whether you will use the wrong terminology. But your worries will most likely be totally overcome once the wedding is underway. Many same-sex couples have a profound faith in God, a faith that has evolved and grown through their personal suffering over many years. Now the day has finally arrived when they will come forward with the one they love, before God and witnesses, to proclaim their love and make their promises for a lifetime. Their joy is sure to fill the sanctuary and, very likely, to warm the hearts of all who have come to the wedding. The way you will feel is very likely going to surprise you.

14. ecumenical & interfaith weddings

THEOLOGICAL REFLECTION
My house shall be a called a house of prayer for all people.
—Isaiah 56:7b

As much as many parents might prefer that their son or daughter marry someone of the same denomination or the same faith, love will have its way! When preparing and performing the wedding, it is good to remember the beautiful words of scripture above because they remind us that God's house and God's love is for all people.

The timbre of the wedding service needs to reflect God's open and unending love.

◼ Protestant & Roman Catholic

It will serve Protestant pastors well to remember that, when Roman Catholic persons are marrying Protestants, the Catholic Church does not want to lose them. In years past, the Protestant member of the couple was required to embrace the Catholic faith. Later, it was only required that the Protestant spouse promise to raise any children from the marriage in the Catholic faith. (This is still the case.) Since the Catholic Church frowns upon members marrying in a Protestant church, when one person of the couple is Catholic, you might want to diplomatically ask why the couple has chosen to be married in a Protestant church. It may simply be, for example, that the bride has grown up in your church and always dreamed of being married there. Or you may find out that the Catholic member would really prefer a Catholic wedding, but just didn't think it was possible. You can explore the options with them.

Some Catholic priests are willing to attend and participate in weddings in Protestant churches, but this will vary from diocese to diocese. Sometimes the marriage can later be "blessed" in a Catholic church. On the other hand, the Protestant member of the couple may be just as happy if the wedding takes place in a Catholic church with you as a representative of that person's faith community in attendance. Occasionally, it is possible for you to participate in some small way in a Catholic service. Although you will not be considered a co-officiant with the priest, you might be permitted to read scripture. Be sure that bride, groom, priest, and you are comfortable with the arrangements and, of course, that what is being done is in accordance with any official rules or unwritten traditions of both churches. You are a representative of your faith tradition and the congregation you serve, and what you are doing needs to be in adherence with the expectations of your office.

All that said, it is essential that a Protestant who is marrying a Catholic understand what the ceremony means in relation to that person's faith. If you are asked to perform a wedding between a Protestant and a Catholic, make sure that the Protestant partner understands that the Catholic partner (officially, at least) is being married for life and, according to the Catholic Church, will never be divorced, even if a divorce takes place according to the law of the land. (Under special circumstances, annulments under Roman Catholic canon law are permitted, but they are difficult to obtain.)

The bottom line is, if a Catholic gets divorced according to the law of the land and marries again, that person is considered by the Catholic Church to be in a state of mortal sin and, therefore, will not be invited to partake in communion until he or she is reconciled with the original spouse, or at least is living a single and celibate life. For this reason, it is important that any serious Roman Catholic who is about to marry a Protestant meet with his or her priest to discuss the issue.

It is also vital to look at the families' positions. Interfaith marriage can bring about strong reactions from family members. Older family members, especially, might have been raised in environments in which intermarriage between Catholic and Protestant was considered scandalous! The adjustment to current norms of diversity is not always easy for them. Parents and grandparents may express disappointment in the choice of a partner. Remind the couple that the waters of faith and tradition run deep, but that their continuing love and sensitivity to the families' feelings will help ease prejudices as time passes.

Couples who are in love and about to be married are generally pretty sure things will work out over the years. Still, it is important that they have some general advance plan about whether they will be a part of one another's faith communities, to what extent, and in which tradition they intend to raise any children.

■ Christian & Jewish

Within Judaism, the covenant relationship of marriage is of primary importance. The Talmud states, for example, that at marriage all sins are forgiven.[1] It is also said that, even though it is illegal within Judaism to sell a Torah scroll, one is allowed to do so if the money is needed to get married.[2] But both Jewish and Christian parents may experience a good deal of discomfort when they first hear that an interfaith marriage is to take place. The reason is rarely a matter of prejudice. It is more likely that the family members are concerned about the difficulties their loved ones may have to face in the days and years ahead.

The members of the Christian family may be thinking about their child's loss of the family rituals related to the faith, such as a traditional church wedding, church attendance at Christmas and Easter, Christmas trees and gift sharing, and grandchildren who will not be angels in the Christmas pageant. What is at stake for the Jewish family—although it, too, includes the issue of rituals and traditions—is more profound. For almost two thousand years, Jews did not have a homeland, and it was their Judaism, not only as a religion but also as culture and tradition, that bonded them as a people. To be Jewish is more than to practice a particular religion. For this reason, and because of the long history of persecution of Jews culminating in the horrors of the Holocaust, Jewish families and Jewish faith communities have a right to be very concerned when their young people choose to marry outside of Judaism. Intermarriage has even been described as a second Holocaust because it results in the loss of so many, including the progeny, from Judaism.

The young couple, because they are in love and for the sake of keeping the peace, will sometimes try to avoid facing these complex issues. They may be relying on the old cliché, "Love will find a way." As the married years go by, however, and especially as children are born to the couple, religious issues inevitably come to the fore, and they will have to be handled. Promises that were made prior to the marriage may be difficult to keep. Any discussions in this regard that can take place in advance of the marriage will be of great help later. If you are a Christian pastor and a Jewish/Christian couple comes to you asking to be married, you have the responsibility to help them address some of these matters:

- What will the interfaith marriage mean to their families of origin?
- What religion have they chosen for their new family that is being created?
- Will one member of the couple convert or will one participate in the other's religious activities?
- In what faith do they plan to raise any children with whom they are blessed?

It may be that the couple has already dealt with these issues in advance of seeking you out for a wedding. At the very least, encourage them to discuss the marriage with a rabbi as well as yourself, and, if things go ahead as planned with you officiating, they may want to invite a rabbi to participate in the service. They may have difficulty, however, locating a rabbi who will assist at a Christian service. They might want to consider a service at a public venue in which you officiate or participate in some way.

If it is settled that the service will be at your church, keep in mind that approximately half of the people attending the ceremony are likely to be Jewish. There are many passages of Christian scripture that can sound quite anti-Semitic or, at the very least, supersessionist. Be careful what Bible readings you choose, and be sure to include passages from Hebrew Scripture. In your choice of New Testament material, there are many passages about love that will be appreciated by both Christian and Jewish people attending the wedding (1 Corinthians 13 is a good choice). There may be people at the service, or members of the wedding party, who have never been inside a church before. Try to make them comfortable with your words of welcome. It might be helpful to take a look at how Jewish wedding services differ, and explain any Christian wedding traditions during the ceremony.

Here is one small detail that could cause some difficulty if not planned in advance. In Christian weddings, it is the tradition for the bride's family to sit on the left side of the center aisle. For Jewish weddings, the tradition is exactly the opposite. You might suggest the Christian tradition be adhered to, if the service is in the church. Better yet, if the couple agrees, why not simply mix the families and guests on both sides?

Remember: Because you were chosen by the couple to perform the wedding and, because you are a Christian pastor, it will be a Christian wedding ceremony. There is no need to apologize or completely remove your religious tradition and language from the service, unless this is something you and the couple have agreed to do. If the wedding was to be neither specifically Jewish nor Christian, then the couple could just as well be married in the county courthouse by a justice of the peace.

Ultimately, a good and successful interfaith marriage will model to the couple's families, community, and world that love indeed conquers all and that God is bigger than any of our human concepts. As families begin to understand each other's traditions, they may even be blessed by them.

■ **cultural considerations**

BRIDE & GROOM OF CULTURES DIFFERENT FROM EACH OTHER

THEOLOGICAL REFLECTION

But Ruth said, . . . "Where you go, I will go; Where you lodge, I will lodge; your people shall be my people, and your God my God. Where you die, I will die—there will I be buried. May the Lord do thus and so to me, and more as well, if even death parts me from you!"—Ruth 1:16–17

True devotion knows no bounds of culture, race, or religion. No families, religious leaders, or cultural expectations can part two people who are determined to be together. Surely Almighty God, who created us out of love and for love, not only understands but blesses pairs who have chosen the permanent devotion to each other described in Ruth. In the case of the Book of Ruth, the devotion is between widowed mother-in-law (Naomi, a Jewish woman) and widowed daughter-in-law (Ruth, a Moabite). Their husbands had died, which in their time and cultures meant there was no protection for them. Ruth chose not only to follow Naomi back to Naomi's homeland but also to claim and worship Naomi's God. Though Ruth may have "converted" when she first married Naomi's son, this new commitment surely required her to change her religion and culture.

When you prepare and perform a wedding where one member of the couple is of a different culture than the other, you will need extreme sensitivity. Get as much information as you can from the one (or both) whose culture is different from your own. Formulate your questions carefully in advance. Some good questions include:

- How do your families each relate to the prospective in-laws and other relatives?
- What is the importance of marriage in each of your cultures?

- Who, in each of your cultures, customarily chooses the partner: the person who is to be married, the parents, or a marriage broker?
- Is there anything I need to know about your culture(s) with which I'm not familiar?

The information you gather will help immensely in preparing a culturally sensitive wedding.

It is important, too, that each member of the couple understands the impact a bi-cultural marriage can have not only on themselves, but also on both families. No doubt, they will have already considered these issues, but it is always good for the couple to articulate them and discuss them together, and with you, in advance of the wedding.

BRIDE & GROOM FROM A CULTURE DIFFERENT FROM THE PASTOR

THEOLOGICAL REFLECTION

The word that came to Jeremiah from the Lord: . . . "For if you truly amend your ways and your doings, if you truly act justly one with another, and if you do not oppress the alien, the orphan, and the widow . . . then I will dwell with you in this place."—Jeremiah 7:1, 5–7

The prophet Jeremiah makes it clear that our goodness to those who are different from ourselves is a high priority of our Creator.

Occasionally, a couple from a culture different from your own will request that you perform their wedding. Perhaps they are new citizens who desire to assimilate into your culture, or they may be visitors. Either way, consider yourself honored to have been asked to participate in this important event of their lives.

If their faith tradition is also different from yours, you might want to ask why they have chosen you and your church, and also make it clear that you will be performing a Christian wedding ceremony. If they belong to another faith, it might be better for them to be married by a religious leader from their own tradition or by a justice of the peace in a secular ceremony—or at least have someone from their religious background in attendance. If it is only a matter of culture but not religion, you still might want to discuss with them the reasons why they are not getting married within their own tradition.

Once this is settled, try to find out as much as is appropriate about what the couple is expecting from the wedding. Then do what you can to meet their needs, while not compromising your own norms. You might want to ask them if there are any words or acts from their culture that could be included as part of the ceremony in order to make both of them and their families feel "at home."

Be sure to go over the words of the wedding service with the couple well in advance of the service so that nobody will be surprised, and they will know what to expect. If there are any language barriers, they might want to engage a translator for themselves or for other family members.

15 weddings in which some are "challenged"

THEOLOGICAL REFLECTION
How beautiful you are, my love, how very beautiful!
—Song of Songs 4:1a

The wedding day is a day when both members of the couple are incredibly beautiful. Needless to say, to the one who loves, the beloved is beautiful every day. Though physical, mental, or emotional challenges dim and disappear in the eyes of love, it is helpful to consider them in preparation for the wedding to give people with these disabilities a high comfort level. Also, some advance preparation will help everyone be able to concentrate on the wedding and not be distracted in any way by the disability.

◼ the deaf & the hearing

Over the years I have had the privilege of teaching in a masters-level biblical studies program specifically for the deaf. I have officiated at a wedding where a good portion of the guests were deaf, although not the bridal couple. I have learned that, in the deaf community, some communicate by ASL (American Sign Language), but that this is not the only sign-type language of the deaf. Also, there are others who receive language better by reading lips.

At the wedding it is important to give those who are deaf the opportunity to follow as much of the ceremony as possible. In order for this to happen, some advance plans will have to be made. If you are accustomed to delivering much of the wedding sermon and the service speaking extemporaneously, you will be well-advised to curb that talent in these circumstances. If you can write out exactly what you will be saying, and give your text in advance to an ASL interpreter, that person will be able to present the text to the deaf as you speak. This way, everyone at the wedding will be able to follow what is being said.

In addition, it is best to have a certain area of the sanctuary roped off for special seating, so that the deaf may sit together with a full view of the interpreter as well as a good sight line to the bridal couple. If only one or two are deaf or if the services of an interpreter are not available, you might want to give guests who are deaf a written copy of the service that they can read in advance of the wedding, or during or after the ceremony.

Needless to say, if one or both of the bridal couple are deaf, an interpreter should be standing alongside you. The service will need to move slowly enough so there is time for the couple to look at each other at various points in the service. You don't want them to have to be looking at the interpreter the entire time!

The couple will exchange their vows and responses in whatever way they are accustomed to communicating with each other, either by speech or by sign. If one or both are using ASL, then the interpreter will speak the words aloud so the congregation can hear them.

▓ the blind & the seeing

When the bride, the groom, or anyone in the wedding party, family, or friends is blind, words become even more important than usual. The way the words are delivered can take on great power. This means that you as pastor will do well to look over what you are going to say and how you will say it, to make the service as beautiful and meaningful in an audio sense as possible. The use of music in such a wedding can also take on a new significance because audio is the primary sense being employed.

The wedding rehearsal can bring some challenges, especially if the blind person is not familiar with your church sanctuary or the location where the wedding is taking place. The blind person will know best what his or her needs are. (Since many legally blind people are able to see to some minimal degree, find out their specific needs.)

The best approach is simply to be sensitive to the issues that are brought forward. Also, if there are blind guests or family members, check with them as to where in the sanctuary they prefer to be seated and how much, if any, assistance they need for entering and exiting.

▓ when some are mentally challenged

If the couple is inviting one or more mentally challenged people to the wedding, or if one or both of the bridal couple is such, then (depending on the condition) it may be important to keep the language of the service relatively simple and straightforward. After you have prepared your wording, check with someone who knows the person well and adjust accordingly it if it appears that there might be any problems.

If there is a family member who is mentally challenged, the couple may want to give that person some kind of needed task to do at the wedding or reception. This will serve as a sign that they value and trust the challenged person, and this person will know that he or she is truly useful. The couple will know best what that task might be: lighting candles, handing out programs, holding the doors open for the bridal party, or any number of other activities. (Refer to Part One for additional ideas.)

◼ when some are physically challenged

It should be possible to include any physically challenged people at the wedding and make them comfortable. If they are in wheelchairs or such, investigate how accessible your church building is. Remember, handicapped people will probably have to be able to go up and down levels, as well as have clear access to bathroom facilities and handicapped-accessible parking spaces, and be able to enter and exit the sanctuary comfortably. If your building cannot accommodate them, you may want to talk with the couple about other possible locations for the ceremony. Or perhaps temporary adaptations can be made, depending on the person's disability. You may have to cordon off a special place for wheelchairs in the sanctuary, in an area that does not violate fire safety codes. It would be good if this is also an area where people will have a clear view of the wedding ceremony.

The best way to help meet the needs of any family or guests who have these special needs is to ask the couple what they think those needs will be and respond accordingly.

16 renewal of vows

Essentially, there are two types of "renewal of vows" ceremonies: for couples who have been estranged and desire to recommit, and for couples who want to honor significant anniversaries. It is somewhat odd that the term "renewal of vows" is used for both; needless to say, the services will be quite different.

◼ for couples who have been estranged

THEOLOGICAL REFLECTION
Then Peter came to him [Jesus] and said to him, "Lord, if another member of the church sins against me, how often should I forgive? As many as seven times?" Jesus said to him, "Not seven times, but I tell you, seventy seven times."—Matthew 18:21–2

When a couple who has been estranged chooses to be rejoined, there is surely rejoicing in heaven! They are clearly obeying Jesus' command that we continue to forgive one another, and that we put no final number on the gift of forgiveness. As Christians, we believe that we are forgiven by God or we would not be able to get through one more day. It is in this forgiveness that we recognize God's unending love. When a couple offers you the opportunity to guide them through a service of forgiveness and renewal of vows, this is a great privilege.

The couple who has been separated is usually coming to you, privately at least, to confess to each other and before a witness (you), and to make an act of forgiveness. Their confession is for any sins of commission, or of omission, that either or both have committed that contributed to their separation. They have also come to proclaim before God and witnesses (maybe just you, or very possibly family and friends), that they are now ready to reunite and be faithful for a lifetime; to love and cherish each other as they had originally promised.

If the couple is not divorced, it is not legally necessary for them to do this. For this reason their choice to do so indicates a deep commitment and should be taken very seriously. They are seeking God's forgiveness and blessing. Accept their confessions at whatever level they choose to share with you (and in whatever form your worship tradition offers) and assure them that they have been forgiven and are given a new chance.

Once you have determined that both members of the couple are truly ready for this renewal of promises, formulate a simple service that will take place before witnesses. They may want a wedding-type ceremony, followed by some kind of dinner or party, or they may want to gather in relative privacy with close family, friends, or both. They may also want family members or friends (who may or may not be the same people as the original bridal party) to stand up with them.

Family members who attend may, at first, be a bit embarrassed if the original breakup was related in some way to infidelity or a similar issue. You can help by simply reminding everyone, in the context of the welcome, that this is a joyous occasion of renewal.

These services can be deeply moving. The couple has often suffered greatly and is grateful for the opportunity and hope that such a service signifies. For a renewal of vows service, I highly recommend the wonderful hymn by Brian Wren entitled "When Love is Found." It is especially appropriate for this occasion. [3]

■ for couples celebrating special anniversaries

THEOLOGICAL REFLECTION
Enjoy life with the wife whom you love, all the days of your vain life that are given you under the sun, because that is your portion in life.
—Ecclesiastes 9:9

To be sure, the book of Ecclesiastes was written by an "older" man, and his reflections sometimes seem negative (such as Ecclesiastes 1:2b, "All is vanity"), but they are clearly the honest reflections of a faithful follower of God. The beautiful thing about the passage above is that it describes the love of a spouse not only as a great gift to be experienced "all the days of your life," but also to "enjoy."

Individuals who have had the privilege of sharing both the joys and the sorrows of human living with a beloved life partner will often want to thank God and to celebrate with their friends on the occasion of an anniversary that is particularly significant. If they have asked you to help facilitate the occasion, you know that the number of years together that they are celebrating is meaningful to them. For a couple who found each other in their forties or later, a twenty-fifth anniversary will be every bit as significant as a fiftieth would be for those who met as a young couple.

Today, as people live longer, you may encounter couples who have been married as much as sixty or even seventy years and are still eager and able to celebrate those years with a religious ceremony and a good party!

People have any number of reasons to want to recite their wedding vows to each other again after decades of marriage, but, for most, this occasion is an opportunity to recall the joys of their youth and their wedding day, and to celebrate their many years together. Besides, what a great excuse for a party! Still, it is more than a party when a service of worship is involved. It is a way of saying thanks to God for the institution of marriage and especially for this marriage.

You may be surprised to learn that "renewal of vows" services can be at least as complicated as wedding services. The couple may have special wedding attire, any number of attendants (sometimes even the original ones) and, in addition, family members, children, grandchildren and greatgrandchildren taking part in the service. There may again be photographers, candles and flowers, even communion. The couple is even likely to ask you to say exactly what the original minister said (usually impossible, even if you were that minister!). Do the best you can, and they will likely be grateful.

Most family members will be in pretty good spirits for this kind of event. As suggested in Part One, there are a variety of opportunities for family to take part, such as reading scripture or offering special music.

17 weddings outside of your church building

Any wedding outside the church building requires some special attention from you, the pastor. For starters, even when relatively traditional, the ceremony should appropriately reflect the space in which that ceremony takes place. In other words, a wedding at a theme park or at pool side are likely to be more relaxed in style than a wedding in your sanctuary.

◼ in a family home or backyard

It is a good idea, when performing a wedding at a family home or in a backyard, to meet with the family whose home it is and look over the setting in advance. Ask yourself the following questions:

- Will my voice be heard in this setting by all who have come to witness the marriage?
- Do I need a microphone and is that an option?

This is an especially difficult problem when you are outdoors. Try to resolve it. Family members will be disappointed if they travel a long distance to the wedding and don't hear a word of it. Sometimes a musician with an electronic organ or piano who is playing for the event will have a microphone you can use. You might need an extension cord. Otherwise, practice your diction and volume, and work on making your voice louder, while still being warm and pleasant. (Any voice teacher or coach can explain how to do this in a lesson or two.) Remember, the bridal couple will still be right in front of you and you don't want to be yelling at them in order to be heard by all!

It is also good to pay special attention to the arrangements for the entrance music for the bridal party and bride. If they have planned nothing in this regard, you might suggest taped music (heaven forbid!), but a responsible adult will have to be assigned to turn the machine on and off at the exact times. Also, the music will have to be programmed and timed appropriately. (This might be a job for a relative who has not been asked to be in the bridal party.)

■ in a hotel, restaurant, or conference center

If the ceremony is taking place in a hotel, restaurant, or conference center, you will probably have access to a sound system, but you will most likely have to request it in advance. One big problem in these places is that there is nearly always some kind of piped-in music playing in the background. It is a fact that the workers rarely know how to turn off that music. Plan in advance for this potential disaster to avoid it!

■ in a wedding chapel

Wedding chapels generally have their own "regulars"—justices of the peace and ministers who perform the ceremonies. Still, there are times you may be asked to perform a wedding in a chapel. The idea of a wedding chapel may not appeal to you in principle, but couples who choose to be married in a wedding chapel are often from out of town and, for various reasons, might not have family or friends attending. If they ask for a pastor, rather than choosing to go to the local courthouse, this is a signal that they are seeking some connection with God in their wedding service. Your willingness to officiate may help provide that connection in some small way.

If you do agree to marry a couple in a wedding chapel, you need to know two things:

- What the couple wants
- What, if any, rules the chapel has

If you are unable or unwilling to comply with both, then you are not the person for the job and simply have to decline. Should you accept the "gig," do your best to show your warmth toward the couple and any people they have invited to attend the wedding. Your efforts are likely to be appreciated beyond measure. Your reward, along with the fee, whatever it may be, will be that you brought a sense of sacredness to a situation that would otherwise have been pretty sterile. You, as a pastor and representative of God, will have been the facilitator of the good memories that began the couple's married life.

◼ on the beach

If you live anywhere near the ocean, you will very likely be asked to perform a wedding or two on the beach. While that may not sound difficult, it can become quite complex. Possible problems include the following: your voice not being heard over the crashing of the waves, having no place to put down your papers or other items, lack of chairs for older people to sit down, or even rain. The worst problem, however, is always the sand. Often at beach weddings, the bridal party has planned to go barefoot, but guests inevitably arrive wearing their very best shoes (not to mention pantyhose!). To add to the troubles, sand has a way of ending up everywhere and in everything. The beach wedding, of course, also can be one of great beauty. If the weather is good, everyone will enjoy the blue skies, the glorious sunshine, the lapping of the waters and, in general, the opportunity to commune with nature.

■ in another church or place of worship

There will, no doubt, be occasions when you are invited to participate at a wedding that is taking place at another church or religious institution. Rule number one is to remember that you are the guest in this situation. As such, you will need to follow the lead of the religious leader of that particular place of worship. Try to know, at least approximately, what is going to be said, and be sure that you are (theologically) comfortable with this marriage, those words, and the role you will take. Also make sure that the bridal couple understands that your role is as a guest leader and representative of the faith community of one member of the couple. You might want to check with the deacons or elders of the church you serve as well, since you will also be representing your church at this wedding.

■ in a place that requires travel

Very occasionally, in the stretch of your life's ministry, you may be asked to perform a wedding in another city, state, or even another country. Your decision to accept will depend on many factors. These include your relationship to the family or families involved, the distance and convenience or inconvenience of the travel, the mode of travel that will be required, and whether your schedule permits (keeping your parishioners' best interests in mind.) There are also financial considerations. However close to the family you may be, it is appropriate that, unless you were going to be in that place anyway, the entire cost be born by those who engage you to officiate. Many pastors have enjoyed a little trip to the Caribbean or to a ski resort or to some such place at the expense of some wealthy family who cannot imagine the wedding being led by anyone else!

Still, even if these seem like great opportunities to travel, these weddings can turn out to be a lot more trouble than they are worth. Is your spouse being invited and paid for as well? Do you really have the time to be away from your regular church responsibilities? How much undone work will be waiting for you when you get home? Do you know many people who will be at the wedding? If you find that you simply can't do this wedding, it is very likely that the family will understand. Everyone knows that pastors are busy people. If you choose to accept, then be well prepared in advance so that you can truly enjoy the trip and the wedding.

A word of caution about officiating at weddings in other states and other countries: It is absolutely necessary that your credentials are in compliance with the legal requirements of the place you will perform the wedding. You will often (for example, if performing a wedding in Canada) be required to prove to the offices of that government that you are an ordained pastor in good standing in a denomination, and you may have to obtain a permit. You might ask the couple to do some of the legwork in this regard, as they will likely have contacts in the area where the wedding is to take place.

As with local weddings in other churches, if the service is to take place in a worship space, be sure you know any requirements of the church and denomination and that you have the approval of the pastor.

■ in any place you least expect

When we pastors get together, our favorite stories are nearly always about weddings and funerals. One recurring topic is the odd places and strange circumstances in which we have performed weddings. Some of these stories are quite unbelievable, ranging from marrying a couple of animal lovers at the zoo to marrying two airline employees at five-thousand feet. You may not have been asked to perform any weddings that are quite this strange, but most pastors have a superb wedding story or two, and you can never be sure when the opportunity will arise!

18 officiating at the wedding of a close family member

◼ performing the wedding of your own child or grandchild

What could be a greater thrill than performing the wedding of your own son, daughter, or grandchild? How could you say no when a beloved child is honoring you by asking you to perform the wedding ceremony? Before you say yes, however, it is important to ask yourself if you have the presence of mind to be both professional pastor and loving parent—at the same time—at your dear one's wedding.

I would venture to say that the most difficult matter in performing the wedding of a family member close to your heart is the issue of tears—your tears. Are you going to be able to keep from crying or getting choked up in the middle of the service in a way that would prevent you from continuing?

When you are both pastor and parent (or grandparent), you will be busy with all the professional details that any wedding entails. Only you know how well you can handle the dual pressures of family and work. Ultimately it is your decision. If you choose to sit back and savor the occasion as (just) a family member, explain your feelings so that your child or grandchild will understand. After all, however called to the ministry and experienced you may be, performing a wedding is still work for you. Let the couple know that, if someone else performs the service, nothing will distract you from fully experiencing the wedding in your primary role as parent or grandparent.

SCENARIO

When Debbie asked her mother, a pastor, to perform her wedding ceremony in a gazebo in a beautiful public park by the lake, her mom was thrilled. However, things became complicated when Debbie also told her mom (whose first career had been as a classical singer) that it had always been her dream that mom sing "Ave Maria" at her wedding. Now mom had three hats! She was to be pastor, mother of the bride, and soprano soloist. Then the so-called organist called to say that he thought there would be no outlet for his electrical piano in the gazebo, and he asked if he could play an accordion instead! Debbie's answer to him was a firm NO. An electrical outlet was located in the gazebo.

When the big day arrived, the breeze off the lake kept blowing the organist's sheet music off the stand. (His wife showed up at the last minute with clothes pegs to hold the music down.) In addition, the chairs had all been set up just a bit too far from the gazebo, and the pastor-mom needed a microphone in order to be heard by everyone. (The organist came to the rescue when he offered his mike with a long cord.) On top of all that, the nephews all had terrible colds, and Grandma was freezing from the chilly wind off the lake.

How did that wedding go? It was the best wedding ever, ever, ever! Every wedding has its glitches, but they mean very little in the long run. All the best parts of that wedding become the memories: the beautiful bride, the fresh clean air, the happy family, and so much more.

■ performing the wedding of your mother or father

THEOLOGICAL REFLECTION
Honor your father and your mother, as the Lord your God commanded you, so that your days may be long and that it may go well with you in the land that the Lord your God is giving you.—Deuteronomy 5:16

You may love your parents and be grateful for their care for all these years, but it can still feel a little strange when a parent asks you to officiate at her or his wedding. Chances are that parent is asking because she or he is very proud that you are a pastor. Your respectful acceptance of this request to perform the wedding would be an excellent way to honor your parent.

How about this one for both a challenge and a joy? As long as you approve of your parent's choice in a new spouse and believe it is a good match, there is nothing to prevent you from officiating at the wedding. If your other parent is still living, however, and you are on loving terms with both parents, it is vital that you have a chat with your other parent before accepting the job. Tell the other parent that you have been asked to perform this wedding and ask this parent how he or she feels about you performing the service. By getting the other parent's blessing, you will keep your relationships intact.

It goes without saying that it is important for the person who is marrying your parent to be totally comfortable with the idea of you performing the wedding. Also be aware that you will be both pastor and son or daughter at the wedding. Any time you are in two roles, there is the possibility of misunderstanding.

Just as with officiating at the wedding of a child or grandchild, the one negative aspect is that you miss the chance to simply sit back, relax, and experience the moment. But a great moment it will be, either way.

19 weddings of "older" couples

It is very likely that, over the duration of your ministry, you will be asked to perform a wedding or two for an "older" couple. (Do keep in mind that, in our culture, no person is described as old or even elderly, only as "older.") Performing a wedding for an older couple will have its special joys and, possibly, its challenges.

Older couples will often want to have a smaller, simpler wedding, sometimes in a home, sometimes in the church with just a few family members and special friends. Many older brides and grooms will be either divorced or widowed. Either way, there are sure to be memories, sweet or bittersweet, of previous weddings. This means that one or the other of the couple may want things done differently this time. Their reasons for doing things a certain way, although often not articulated (or sometimes, not even realized), may be related to their memories of their first wedding. So, try as best you can to meet their requests for the wedding ceremony while being faithful to your own theologies and any regulations of your denomination and congregation.

Older couples often want to write their own vows. This may be partly to ensure that they are different from their original vows to an earlier spouse. Or the couple may want to express their love by making vows that refer in some way to the maturity or life experience they are bringing into this new relationship. If they are writing their own vows, be sure that they are still making the lifetime promises that a marriage is all about; faithfulness in times of sickness and health, wealth and poverty, for better or for worse and, of course, until death.

One issue you may have to deal with is that of adult children—of either the bride or the groom, or of both—who do not approve of the marriage.

SCENARIO

John and Marian had been married for thirty years and, just after their children were raised and gone, Marian became ill. During the ten years that Marian was in and out of hospital, there was one special home health nurse, Lorraine, who became the most helpful friend of them both. When Marian passed away, it was only a matter of months before John and Lorraine were meeting for coffee, feeling drawn to each other by their memories of Marian and of the struggle they had shared. Eight months after Marian's death, John and Lorraine decided to get married.

The community and close friends kept their thoughts to themselves, but John's two grown daughters were devastated. They did not want to attend the wedding because, as they said to their (then also devastated) father, they felt that attending this wedding would be an insult to their beloved mother.

The pastor was called in to try to help. After some counseling with all parties, the pastor explained to John and Lorraine that his daughters loved him, but that they were grieving deeply over their mother. He then explained to the daughters that their father loved them, but that he did have the option of moving forward in his life. Their dear mother was gone, but their father was alive. If they loved him, perhaps they would choose in time to try to understand. Yes, John, as a relatively new widower, may have been attracted to another woman too soon. But he had, after all, cared for his wife over the years of her illness right to the end. Now he was legally free to remarry, and this was his choice. His decision to marry again was not *against* his first wife, even though the wedding was taking place far too soon for his daughters' liking.

The family sat down together and talked. The daughters, in the end, chose to attend the wedding. It took them two or three years before they began to feel comfortable with their father's new wife, Lorraine, but in time, because they did love their father, they began to see her qualities.

Adult children might not approve of the marriage of the older couple for any number of reasons. Sometimes their worries are emotional, but other times they are related to financial issues. Could a new spouse come in and possibly inherit everything? If this seems to be the case, their concerns can often be dissipated if the couple chooses to arrange for a prenuptial agreement. This may seem callous at the time. Still, if one considers that it has taken a lifetime to build a financial legacy, it may not be fair that a new spouse become the full beneficiary. The funds were very likely accrued during the first marriage and with the help of the first spouse. A prenuptial agreement allows each person's assets or a portion of them to go to his or her first family. Marriage later in life might be for love, or even appropriately for companionship, but it should never be just about money. On the other hand, the new spouse will also need to have enough money to be protected at the time of the partner's death. While financial issues are the couple's own business and not those of the pastor, it is still good to be aware of the matter.

The older couple may want to have adult daughters or sons stand up with them, and it is completely appropriate for these adult children to serve as maids or matrons of honor and best man, or even give the bride in marriage.

One final issue needs to be addressed. Occasionally, older couples will ask a pastor to officiate at a wedding without the benefit of any legal documents. The reason for this is that, under some circumstances, legal marriage would cause them to lose individual financial benefits that they are currently receiving from the government. It is, of course, your own decision as to whether to perform such a "wedding." Still, do keep in mind that, although the church does not always agree with what the government is doing, it is important that, as professionals of integrity in the community, we pastors do not intentionally engage in any activity that could be conceived as breaking the law or assisting others in doing so. It is also required that we work within the framework of our own denomination and its regulations in this regard. We are not lone wolves, but part of an operating system that we represent as clergy.

* * *

Well, pastor, now you are ready to receive and respond positively to that initial call to your office from just about any prospective bride or groom. You are also prepared for almost anything that might happen as you and the couple work together through the preparation for the wedding, the wedding, and the reception.

Still, let's spend a little more time together. You may have some concern about those pesky wedding sermons. They need to have theological content. They need to be personal. They need to be short! And they always come up as an extra sermon you have to produce in addition to your Sunday sermon, so time is often of the essence. Part Four will address the issue of the wedding sermon.

part four

the wedding sermon

The section includes suggestions and examples of wedding sermons or meditations. Needless to say, if you adapt any of these ideas, you will need to adjust as appropriate for:

- the specific couple
- your thoughts, faith, and style
- setting and size of the wedding
- the people who will be present

In other words, you might give a rather different sermon if you know that a large number of the people coming to the wedding will be younger, older, or from a different faith community. Also, if there are specific family issues you know about, you may want to indirectly address the issue(s). It is sometimes possible to diffuse problems by good words spoken in the context of a short wedding sermon.

THEOLOGICAL REFLECTION
Proclaim the message; be persistent whether the time is favorable or unfavorable; convince, rebuke, and encourage, with the utmost patience in teaching.—2 Timothy 4:2

Yes, there may be some people at the wedding who look forward to enjoying the sermon you will offer. Others may be distracted or even annoyed at anything that, in their opinion, holds up the proceedings. At some weddings there may even be people who are unfamiliar with the sermon format. Yet, you are called to preach both in and out of season, or, as it says in Second Timothy, "whether the time is favorable or unfavorable." You might as well enjoy preaching. Keep it short and be sure the message is the best it can be. Keep it specifically focused on the couple you are about to marry.

20 sermon samples & ideas

■ "God is love"

(idea for a sermon on 1 John 4:4–12)

Beloved, let us love one another, because love is from God; everyone who loves is born of God and knows God. Whoever does not love does not know God, for God is love. God's love was revealed among us in this way: God sent his only Son into the world so that we might live through him. In this is love, not that we loved God but that he loved us and sent his Son to be the atoning sacrifice for our sins. Beloved, since God loved us so much, we also ought to love one another. No one has ever seen God; if we love one another, God lives in us, and his love is perfected in us.—1 John 4:7–12

This passage from First John tells the couple and all those gathered (churched and unchurched) some very important things about God. First, it says that love is from God, and that if we love, we know God. Second, it offers a basic Christian faith statement about the identity of Christ. Third, it reminds us that the gift of Christ is a love gift and that loving each other is an appropriate response to this free gift, a response that is pleasing to God.

If you know there will be wedding guests of other faiths or no faith, a selected portion of this passage also works well:

Beloved, let us love one another, because love is from God; everyone who loves is born of God and knows God. Whoever does not love does not know

God, for God is love. . . . No one has ever see God; [but] if we love one an-
other, God lives in us, and his love is perfected in us.—I John 4:7–8, 12

The advantage of this shortened version is that it points out
in absolutely simple and clear language that if we know love, we
know something of God, because God *is* love. Because the focus of
the wedding is that two people have chosen love, everyone at the
wedding, whatever their faith or lack of it, is likely to be touched
by this very good news that love is a gift from God.

■ "goals for a lifetime"

First Corinthians 13 is a popular passage that everybody seems to
love hearing at a wedding. These words will ring with truth and
beauty for every person present at the wedding, whatever the person's faith background.

> *If I speak with the tongues of mortals and of angels, but do not have love, I*
> *am a noisy gong or a clanging cymbal. And if I have prophetic powers, and*
> *understand all mysteries and all knowledge, and if I have all faith, so as to*
> *remove mountains, but do not have love, I am nothing. If I give away all*
> *my possessions, and if I hand over my body so that I may boast, but do not*
> *have love, I gain nothing. Love is patient; love is kind; love is not envious or*
> *boastful or arrogant or rude. It does not insist on its own way; it is not irrita-*
> *ble or resentful; it does not rejoice in wrongdoing, but rejoices in the truth. It*
> *bears all things, believes all things, hopes all things, endures all things. Love*
> *never ends. But as for prophesies, they will come to an end; as for tongues,*
> *they will cease; as for knowledge, it will come to an end. For we know only*
> *in part, and we prophesy only in part; but when the complete comes, the*
> *partial will come to an end. . . . And now faith, hope, and love abide, these*
> *three; and the greatest of these is love.—I Corinthians 13:1–10, 13*

Isn't it wonderful to hear these words of the Apostle Paul
from First Corinthians describing the ideal of what it means to
love? On the other hand, who among us could honestly say that we
meet all those requirements, all those attributes on that incredible

list? "Love is patient; love is kind; love is not envious or boastful or arrogant or rude. Love does not insist on its own way; it is not irritable or resentful; it does not rejoice in wrongdoing." In the course of a lifetime relationship, there are times when most of us have been impatient, unkind, envious, or boastful. There are certainly days when we have wanted our own way and probably a lot of days when we have found ourselves feeling irritable. (Not today, of course!) While we might have *some* of those attributes of love *some* of the time, not many of us could say we behave that way every day.

When Paul offered this list about love to the people of Corinth, it is quite possible that he was pointing out these qualities as *goals* rather than achievements, since he preceded the passage with the statement, "But strive for the greater gifts" (1 Corinthians 12:31a). _____ and _____, in your marriage and in your lives ahead of you, neither of you is likely to be perfect because none of us are perfect—or even anywhere near. We are human. But when two people truly love each other, there is understanding and there is forgiveness.

Forgiveness is one of the great gifts of God and one of the gifts that those who love can give to each other. It is in loving, in trying and making mistakes and then forgiving and trying again, that our lives unfold. Of course, when people truly love, they never want to hurt each other by making mistakes. But it is in the good and the not-so-good that life brings that a couple truly becomes, as the Bible says, "one flesh." And God will be with you in the trying.

There will also be many times in your life together that you will exhibit these wonderful attributes of patience and kindness toward each other. Individually, as a couple, and as a family, you will also reach out to others and to your community and world, demonstrating these same qualities. You will be part of making a better world when you do these good things.

Paul goes on to say that love "bears all things, believes all things, hopes all things, and endures all things." Your marriage is about hope and trust. You will not only put up with each other's foibles and mistakes, but you will truly believe in each other as your lives progress. To believe in each other is to have the trust and expectation that each of you is trying to be the best he or she can be, and to support each other's dreams and choices in life.

As you live your lives together, as you work toward these goals of love, remember, too, that God's love and presence is reflected through your relationships with other people. These who have gathered to celebrate with you today, your beloved families and friends, can often reflect the love of God for you. Let them love and care for you. Love them back as God would have you do. Try your best to be gentle and kind and patient. Live your lives together remembering, as Paul says, that "faith, hope and love abide, these three; and the greatest of these is love."

■ "three in the house: God with us"

Today is your wedding day. Today you see the very best in each other. You will also enjoy the company of your friends and family. You will celebrate, laugh, and maybe even cry with joy, and revel in the incredible happiness that love can bring. And then you will go home together to live "happily ever after." Well, you *will* live together and you *will* have happiness, but as we all know, life has a way of bringing a fair number of challenges as well. The usual mix includes annoyances and difficulties, sometimes financial troubles, and sometimes illnesses, not to mention dealing with worries about the mess the world has gotten itself into in our time. Life is never simple, and it is into this real world that you two now enter —together. Now you two are one. Now you have a support system, a perfect "one" that is blessed by God. You will be there for each other, no matter what happens, and that is one of the purposes of marriage.

Today I urge you both to remember this. You do not go into this marriage alone. First of all, your friends and family go with you. They won't be at your home every day, but their hearts and minds and prayers are with you, and for your marriage. That is why so many of them are here with you today to celebrate. Their presence is their way of offering their blessing on your union. These people are on your side.

These friends and family are not the only ones devoted to the success and happiness of your marriage. There is also God. God goes with you into this marriage, from this day forward. *The Book of Common Prayer* puts it this way: "Marriage is an honorable estate, ordained by God." Whether or not you pray daily, God is with you daily. Whether or not you attend church regularly, God is with you regularly. Whether or not things are going smoothly, God is with you. God's love will follow you both, wherever you go, whatever you do.

It will be good if you remember God, if you remember to pray together, worship together, raise any children in the faith, and trust in God to get you through everything. These practices will help nourish your marriage through years of both good and bad. Remember that, whatever you do, the God who created you will support and nourish you. God wishes you well. Keeping this in mind and in your heart will help and guide you through the challenges life brings.

Today you have come to the church and to God, asking that your marriage be holy and blessed. Today God does bless your union. Whatever life may bring, there will be at least three at your house: the two of you and God. Like a loving parent, God is with you. Like a teacher and guide, God prods and urges you on to do good for others.

So, be very good to each other. Model this love of God that you know through Jesus. Model a love that is forgiving and kind, a love that is gentle and respectful. Marriage is a great privilege and not to be taken for granted. You have found each other, and your love is a precious gift from God, one of the greatest of all gifts. And remember, for all time, God is with you today and always.

◼ "love is strong"
(sample sermon on Song of Solomon 8:6–7)

Set me as a seal upon your heart, as a seal upon your arm;
for love is strong as death, passion fierce as the grave.
Its flashes are flashes of fire, a raging flame.
Many waters cannot quench love, neither can floods drown it.
If one offered for love all the wealth of his house,
it would be utterly scorned.
—Song of Solomon 8:6–7

_____ and _____, today is your wedding day. To-day you make your promises before God and these witnesses. You make these promises because you love each other. Right now, your love is strong. On this day you truly understand the words of the biblical book Song of Solomon, that you are setting one another as a seal upon your heart. Today your love is stronger than death, a love so deep and strong that it cannot be quenched.

All those who are gathered to celebrate with you are here to show that they wish for you a love that will go on this way for a lifetime together. Your family and your friends wish for you a love that will continue through all the difficulties that life can and surely will bring. But many are also aware that time and the trials of life have often damaged, and even destroyed, the love of many couples who started out just like you.

Why is it that some marriages fall on rocky ground while others grow and thrive? A lot of people will tell you that it is hard work that makes a marriage survive and helps the love relation-ship grow. That is all well and good, but I'd like to suggest some other ways to have a happy marriage for a lifetime. First of all, re-member and hold onto the love you feel today. Take these mo-ments, great moments in your personal histories, and hold them close to your hearts. Over the years, talk with each other about to-day and about the good times. Share with each other the memories most precious to you. Treasure them.

The second way to nurture your love, when the troubled times come—as they inevitably do—is to cling to each other. Trust each other. Support each other. Tell each other "I love you" and "I appreciate you." Listen to each other's problems. You truly need to be each other's best friend.

There is one more key to a successful, lifelong marriage: Re-member that you are not alone. You have all these wonderful peo-ple gathered here to wish you well. They have promised today to support your marriage. Know that they are _for_ you. And God is with you and for you as well. In all the days of this marriage, God will support your great love.

The Bible passage you heard from Song of Solomon says that love is strong as death, and that no person would give up love for any amount of wealth. The love you share today, and that love as it grows, is and always will be the most precious possession you could ever have. Treasure and nurture that love. May your marriage be truly blessed.

■ "becoming one flesh"
(sample sermon on Genesis 2:22–25)

Today you two wonderful people are being married. Even though you may have made the decision together some time ago, today is the day you become, as the Bible says, "one flesh." This means that your hopes and dreams are not only for yourselves but for each other. Your desires and your prayers will be each for the other. Your plans for the days and years ahead will be quite different from what they might have been if you were single.

Although many people have fine and useful lives as singles, still, we continue to stand in awe of the wonder of the gift of marriage. Marriage means that two people have opened their hearts to love, and then have chosen to open their lives to trust each other above all others. Marriage means that there is someone you care for even above yourself, although you must also care for yourself as a good and loving partner.

There is a very beautiful passage about marriage in the Bible, in the book of Genesis, the first book of the Bible. Its purpose in the context of a story is to tell us about God creating the earth. It says that God made human beings not to be alone, but to be together. As the story goes, God takes a rib from the one and then uses it to create the other. So it is not surprising that the man, when he first sees the woman, after having looked at and named all the animals, says, "This, at last, is bone of my bones and flesh of my flesh!" (Genesis 2:23a). You may remember such a moment in your relationship when, whether or not words were spoken, you discovered that the other was not really "other" at all, but part of your true being.

God has done something wonderful. God has made us for each other. What a gift this is from a loving God, that we should find our true mate for life and come to realize that! This is what we all celebrate today—that love between the two of you.

The Genesis passage goes on to say, "Therefore a man leaves his father and his mother and clings to his wife and they become one flesh" (Genesis 2:24). It is interesting to note that, at the time this passage was written, it would have always been the woman who left her parents and went to live with her husband. We cannot know for sure the reason it is said here that it is the man who must leave father and mother. The point, however, is that it is God's will that the man cleaves or clings to his wife. The message makes it clear that husband and wife, wife and husband, are a family that becomes the primary family for both. Of course, each of you will continue to love your family of origin, parents and siblings, grandparents, and all your relatives. But your primary responsibility and accountability, your primary hopes and dreams and life, will, from this day forward, be tied to each other. You are a brand new family and, whether that family continues to be just the two of you, or whether it multiplies over the years, today is Day One of this beautiful new family.

As you go out into the world as a married couple, remember also that you two will be given the privilege of serving others. Cling to each other, but not so much that you are not able to reach out to others both for help and for giving of yourselves. Together you will be stronger. Together you will be better. Together you will know that you always have consolation. Thank God every day for the gift God has given you today, the gift of love and of marriage. God blesses marriage. As *The Book of Common Prayer* says, "Marriage is an honorable estate; ordained by God." Remember this and you will be able to celebrate the gift of marriage every day of your lives together. May God bless your marriage today, the first day, and every day to come."

■ conclusion

As we have considered throughout this book, weddings are great
and life-changing occasions, but they are not always easy for us as
pastors! Our calendars are nearly always full, and weddings inevitably result in more work and more hours added to already hectic
schedules. Still, performing weddings can also be incredibly satis-
fying. When things go well, and when we can see new family relationships being created and memories of a lifetime being made, we
feel good. At the end of the day, we pastors can find real joy in this
part of our work. We have the privilege of being a small part of a
celebration in the lives of two families, as well as in the creation of
a new family. That's a good part of what ministry is all about.

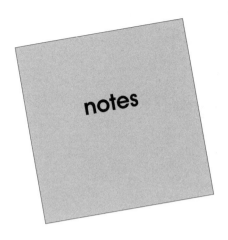

notes

part one: preparation for the wedding

1. Snyder, Graydon F., and Doreen M. McFarlane, *The People Are Holy: The History and Theology of Free Church Worship.* (Macon, GA: Mercer University Press, 2005), 86.

part two: the wedding day

1. Snyder and McFarlane, *The People Are Holy,* 88.
2. Ibid., 88.

part three: special circumstances

1. *The Talmud,* Yeb.63a ; Yer.Bik.iii.3.
2. *The Talmud,* Meg.27a:Yer.Bik.iii.6.
3. "When Love Is Found" by Brian Wren, *New Century Hymnal,* Cleveland, OH: Pilgrim Press, 1995. Words © 1983 by Hope Publishing Company.

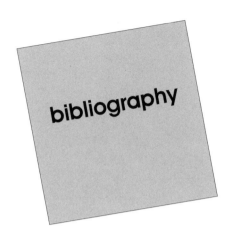

bibliography

Davies, K. C., and the experts at GayWeddings.com. *The Complete Guide to Gay and Lesbian Weddings*. New York: St. Martin's Press, 2005.

Ellison, Marvin M. *Same-Sex Marriage: A Christian Ethical Analysis*. Cleveland, OH: The Pilgrim Press, 2004.

Hagen, Shelly. *The Everything Wedding Book: The Ultimate Guide to Planning the Wedding of Your Dreams* (3rd ed.). Avon, MA: Adams Media Corporation, 2004.

Kaplan, Jane. *Interfaith Families: Personal Stories of Jewish-Christian Intermarriage*. West Port, CT: Praeger Publishers, 2004.

Knox Beckius, Kim. *The Everything Outdoor Wedding Book*. Adams Media Corporation, 2005.

Myers, David G., and Letha Dawson Scanzoni. *What God Has Joined Together? A Christian Case for Gay Marriage*. San Francisco: HarperSanFrancisco, 2005.

Oakley, Mark, ed. *Readings for Weddings*. London: SPCK, 2004.

Say, Elizabeth A., and Mark R. Kowalewski. *Gays, Lesbians, and Family Values*. Cleveland, OH: The Pilgrim Press, 1998.

Snyder, Graydon F., and Doreen M. McFarlane. *The People Are Holy: The History and Theology of Free Church Worship*. Macon, GA: Mercer University Press, 2005.

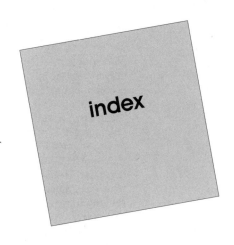

index

scripture
index

Other Books from The Pilgrim Press

FIRST COMES LOVE?: The Ever-Changing Face of Marriage
JOHN C. MORRIS
ISBN 978-0-8298-1755-3/paper/112 pages/$12.00

> In an entertaining yet factual manner, Morris explores 21 different traditions of marriage in our biblical, European, North American heritage.

HOW TO SUCCEED IN MARRIAGE: The Looking Up Series
ISBN 0-08298-0750-0/paper/24 pages/$3.00

> A short, yet concise booklet that shares words of wisdom on how to have a successful marriage.

BECOMING A MULTICULTURAL CHURCH
LAURENE BETH BOWERS
ISBN 0-8298-1704-2/paper/240 pages/$24.00

> Bowers reflect upon and shows how churches can benefit from the experience of First Congregational Church of Randolph, Massachusetts. Once a historically "traditional" one social grouping church, First Congregational is now a "multicultural" church and one of the numerically largest churches in Randolph.

CAN THIS CHURCH LIVE?: A Congregation, Its Neighborhood, and Social Transformation
DONALD MATTHEWS
ISBN 0-8298-1648-8/paper/112 pages/$14.00

> This resource chronicles the story of a church that had an opportunity to thrive in the midst of a community that greatly changed it demographics. Matthews directs readers through the painful process he experienced with the pastor and church leaders as they faced a harsh dilemma—can or will a predominately white church embrace and welcome the people of color who live within the community?

HOW TO GET ALONG WITH YOUR CHURCH: Creating Cultural Capital for Ministry
GEORGE B. THOMPSON JR.
ISBN 0-8298-1437-X/paper/176 pages/$17.00

> This resource incorporates Thompson's research and observations on pastoring a church. He finds that the pastors who are most successful in engaging their parishioners are the ones who develop "cultural capital" within their congregations, meaning that they invest themselves deeply into how their church does its work and ministries.

GIFTS OF MANY CULTURES: Worship Resources for the Global Community
Maren C. Tirabassi and Kathy Wonson Eddy
ISBN 0-8298-1029-3/paper/336 pages/$20.00

> This book is a moving collection of liturgical resources from the global community that is designed to enrich the worship life of congregations in all denominations. It is an anthology of original prayers, stories and readings for sermons, invocations, calls to worship, confessions, and others resources that can be used around the seasons of the church year.

To order these or any other books from The Pilgrim Press call or write to:
The Pilgrim Press
700 Prospect Avenue East
Cleveland, Ohio 44115-1100
Phone orders: 1-800-537-3394 • Fax orders: 216-736-2206

> Please include shipping charges of $4.00 for the first book and $0.75 for each additional book. Or order from our web sites at www.pilgrimpress.com and www.ucpress.com. Prices subject to change without notice.